Wynne Francis
Sir George Williams
University.

Atlantis

Atlantis

LOUIS DUDEK

DELTA CANADA
Montreal 1967

Published by Delta Canada, 3476 Vendome Avenue, Montreal, Canada.
Distributed in the United States by Unicorn Press, Santa Barbara, California.
Parts of this poem have appeared in **Tamarack Review, Yes, Island, The Canadian Author and Bookman,** and selections have been read on radio for the Canadian Broadcasting Corporation. Grateful acknowledgment is made to these journals and media.
The author also wishes to express thanks to the Canada Council for a grant in 1961 which made the writing of the poem possible.
Book cover and design by Allan Harrison.

PROLOGUE

Of voyages : there was Ulysses' voyage,
and Cortez, the great adventurers.

But even suburban dwellers
voyage, though they commute, eat toast, get their magazines
                                                    on time
even a beggar in front of Morgan's
voyages on his worn-out magic carpet of cold.

The voyage is still the prototype —
touristic now, because we city people
                    do not slosh through blood
but live in glass observation cars of boredom.

One could not write a poem waiting for the train to start.
But once in motion, well in motion
how is it possible not be begin ?

Travel is the life-voyage in little,
            a poem, a fiction, structure of illusion !
And then you ask, 'What does it mean ?'

Voices, baggage, a girl's knee,
            and bells, distant, obscure
Every object a word, language, the record we make
a literal transcription,
                then a translation
into moral, abstract meaning.

Travel, to and from (the place does not matter)
            the Ding an sich in a mirror —
Let it speak !

Anyone who travels
            sees others at the crossroads.
There is more than one road.

Who knows where the others may lead to ?

There are infinite worlds : green lights,
                              highway lines, homes,
power stations and industrial domes.

All these things are other people's lives,
effective symbols of their discovered desires.

And what new road lies ahead ? What
              out of our living centre may we not create ?

(I can be as cynical as the rest of them.
It is more difficult to reconstruct these illusions
              than to destroy them.)

But to write poetry in a crowd of people ?
The self is drowned. A 'lost illusion'.
When illusion itself is blurred —
                    are we nearer to reality ?

          Chaos !
A bad knee, or neuralgia,
less real when everything is clear
        than chaos which is alive, like that dime
that rolled along the floor —
                    "A living thing."

Too many illusions
blur Pietro, Carbuio, Stefano and me into a oneness.
              A chaos of Italian
prepares a renaissance,
              at least of wonder !

How seagulls know what they are !

So to be, whatever you are —
          a white bird,
                    a man with a blue guitar.
But there is room for more, more.

It is the part of us
not yet finished as seagull or man

that worries us at the pit of creation,

hanging over cliffs, drowning,
                or lifted in flight

to new states of being, asking always what we are.

Like this ship leaving, gently, to silent tears
                falling all around,
the infinite poem begins, with its power
        of a great ocean-liner greeting the waves,
bound for the sea, its home.

So the waves of the sea (it all comes back to me
                as when I first heard it),
the white snowcaps breaking,
the power of repetition, multitudes,
like the universe of atoms —

ephemeral, too, the making and breaking
                                of crested forms.

It comes back to me
        (like a wave in these waters)
in the repetition of these lines.

I will tell you what it is with the society of ship-folk.

They make the effort to mix, out of baser elements,
        the cheap coin of their private lives,
a new reality, but cannot

(forget those who want a good time,
        are young and pretty and find it).

It is here that the dentist, the lawyer, the housewife,
                the teacher,
try to meet for the first time
        hoping to be made into something new.

"A man should be free"
          "I never interfere with my sons, never !"
"You should forget about money . . ."

Are bored (the lawyer is bored with the dentist,
          the dentist is bored with the teacher) :
their structured selves stick out,
          as lawyer, doctor, housewife, clerk

(forget the young, who have no past to shatter,
                              who want a good time
and take it in any form).

The middle-aged want a new life, but do not find it,
                              not on this voyage.
Perhaps they think that death will be a new reminting.

One never knows about people.
The gay ones we started with
have come up with secret illnesses, private griefs ;
lovely girls proved dull, selfish, or vain,
the scholarship winner a tongue-tied boy.

But the middle-aged one might have ignored
                              one cannot now forget.

The dark lady who told me she was never entirely at home,
in Italy or in America,

and the Albanian whose language we explored —
          Perendy for God,
                    shurf for death.

There are some whose talk is salty and seasoned,
who do not care at all for what you say.

They've found their way, and will not be changed
for pleasure or loud mercurial chatter.

These corals are excellent samples,
          the end, perhaps, of long searching and care.

(Lukewarm Canadians! As if anything but the extremes
                of any ideal were worth a damn . . .

What you want is not 'compromise'
                but a powerful combination of virtues!)

Speaking of coral, the white whirling wave
behind the ship
is like a Japanese painting of a wave.

It is not the painting that is like a wave
but the wave like a real painting —
as exact, as detailed, as white and delicate,
made of many tiny hands, of drops, of lacing lines,
a continuous flocculation of white light
that is unlike mere water as a Rembrandt is unlike mere paint.

That nature is the prime artist does not mean that
                all nature is art.
The means are wasteful, but the occasional fragment
may be a masterpiece, a poem, or even a man.

Chatter is like churning water,
                a formless deformation of words.

Real speech, some eloquence,
                demands an occasion —
a ritual (today is Palm Sunday).

It seems so easy
but about a page or so a day is what it comes to —
                no more. Sometimes better.

The search for meaning's a sudden compacting
of thought that took maybe days or years —
the poem a crystal
                formed in an empty cave of time.

And it would be far more difficult, almost impossible,
to write a poem in the rhythm of another, earlier, poem
than to write a new one, in the rhythm of a new one.

Reading in passage, in mid-ocean, in the midst of Italian
people,

Silone, and Rostovtzeff on Rome,
the real Italians chattering, the real cafoni,
          with *sciocchezza* and *chiacchiera* on either side,
neither cute numskulls nor comic innocents
          as depicted in the tradition
they are of all kinds :
Rostovtzeff tells their earliest history
          (blood flowing through the arches of the Colosseum).

Roman history is a tale of snarls and murderous fangs,
          greed forever impelling the extortionist's hand.
The Gracchi only accelerated the super-state
          crashing toward absolutism.
                    (Can we arrest it ?
          Provide a program — of "Order and Freedom"?)

One learns that great evil, like great good,
          is not the property of any people,
                    but is a monopoly of the state —
or a disease of noble minds corrupting desire.
These Italians were already subjugated under Rome ;
for them the Gracchi spoke, the slaves revolted and failed.
They are the remnants of the oppressed through time.
Of those who survive, few were masters, most
          are born paupers. They suffered and here they are.

If you want to know what the "Class system" really is
          take a sea voyage.
Same as on land, in cities,
only more legibly defined :
          Limit of the Third Class,
                    sour oranges,
          lousy films (first run features are being shown
                    in the First Class),
          poor service, cheap wine.

Same as on land, where money
chalks out the limit of the Third Class —

                    restaurants you do not go to,
                              smart hotels,
                    food you do not buy, entertainments,
                    bad service and wine,
                    cheap tenements.

An ocean voyage
can be a lesson in politics and economics, as well as love.

I suppose the Russians will make the revolution —
                    a classless ship !

We're looking for chaos, the laws of freedom,
where there is so much failure, of concretion,
                    and petrifaction.

I can hardly see the white light or the flow of foam
through the black pigments and structure of matter.

If one could always leave a ship, an old mess,
as easily as this one ...
But we continue, dragging our failures,
                    like excrements, behind us.
As if there were not enough fresh substance, uncreated,
          to mould into new being.

Though we must build on the past, like the genes,
and nature in us is limited (since nothing
                    comes of nothing),
everything still can be made of what is there.
The multiplicity of chaos, our actual lives
whatever they are, leaves us
free to take the pieces, in any order, and move
                    with new desires.

"I hate travel"
but all the poetry I've ever written seems to be about travel.

9

Like this voyage ... (all life's a voyage
        and any small voyage is a lifetime in little).

Leisure and pleasure (whatever that is)
        test even one's capacity for boredom —
the calcified clinkers of other men's minds.

One "passenger" is a former Fascist soldier
        in the armies of Mussolini,
surrendered in Sicily, taken prisoner

to America, married to a U.S. citizen.

Now, sixteen years later, himself an American,
he is returning to Italy as a visitor.

Italian politics doesn't interest him,
his conversation is very dull.

He is burdened with a drab dumpy wife
        that he exchanged for his army record.

His real identity is buried in the Libyan sands.

Today we passed over Atlantis,
        which is our true home.
We live in exile
waiting for that world to come.

Here nothing is real, only a few
        actions, or words,
bits of Atlantis, are real.

I do not love my fellow men
        but only citizens of Atlantis,
or those who have a portion
of the elements that make it real.

One day at sea, at sunset,
            when the long rays struck the water,
it seemed to me the whole sea was living
                        under the surface motion ;

the waves moved like a great cosmic animal
twisting and turning its muscular body
under the grey glistening skin.

And I thought that land also is such a body.
and all men, and all living things —
the life within made invisible, or hardened,
                or covered with deep hard crust,

until it is scraped or dug for, or cleared away,
or with love reached, or by art or other good,
                        seen for a moment —

like a great cosmic animal, of great power, of great beauty.

Eidolons, visions of that reality
            in moments of illumination,
are the things we love.

Librarians would never conquer an empire,
but power, the aggrandizing ego, having conquered,
the universal librarians may follow.

What if it conquers an empire of librarians ?
This also has happened.

It is a matter of destiny, whether one is partnered
with the conquerors or the conquered.

Today we have two, neither entirely barbarous,
having one root and one stem : Liberty, Equality,
growing out of Fraternity.

Demonic power, at war, may destroy mankind.
The libraries totter. And they will fall
unless the powers learn to yield to an encompassing peace.

The question is not whether America has liberty or whether
                                                        Russia
                    has equality ;
it's what they aim at.
The question is whether either really rejects the other.

The last girl I was in bed with
                    was very gentle and kind.
She knew the bodily peculiarities.
We sat talking quietly for half an hour,
                              then love began.

True lovers are wonderfully generous and kind.

Those who cannot love
                    prohibit love to others.
But the will to power is fury
                    against the need to love.

These hours are of no interest —
                    I sit and stare.
Wait for the words to come.

They appear with new perception, a flash of light,
mere words — "A wonderful voyage ..." "Monkeys !"
                              (at Gibraltar) —
or you hear "mare nostrum" in the air.

I go to drink coffee, expecting nothing,
hoping that the gods are kind.

Conquest by force is possible,
                    but real conquest is moral.
If there is no superior life to bring in there is no victory,
or the conqueror himself may be overcome.

Marble is the cross-section of a cloud.
What, then, if the forms we know
                    are sections of a full body
whose dimensions are timeless
                    and bodiless, like poems,
whose unseen dimension is mind ?

I want to learn how we can take life seriously,
        without afflatus, without rhetoric ;
to see something like a natural ritual,
            maybe an epic mode unrevealed,
in the everyday round of affairs.

The touch of land, solid under sea-legs,
touch of the present
                no matter how sad or poor.
Even in ignorance, to have something we can believe in
                        to stand on.
To join in the crowd.

I was never so moved to imagine
                    the alternatives of being
as in the midst of the sea's commotion —
                        the clouds and wave-rolls
out of which these islands are formed
            like porphyritic stones under Vesuvius.

But land is delightful
After an interval of dreaming, of vertigo,
                            of suspension,
to walk again on soil, the sand
on which our cities and ephemeral homes are built.

I

"*Il n'arrive pas à beaucoup d'hommes de retrouver dans le réel, à portée de leur regard, ce monde que la plupart ne découvrent qu'en eux-mêmes quand ils ont le courage et la patience de se souvenir.*"

FRANÇOIS MAURIAC

1

How I hated my first look at Naples
          (having taken the wrong streets).
Then I saw the fringes of its variety,
walking till my legs were aching...

And sat down at a *Ristorante*
          to eat sea-food

(never ate such succulent cooking —
baked mussels, fish, oysters, clams etc.
          and sops of bread in hot sauce).

I have reconciled myself to reality,
I am prepared to be engaged.

...What pained my greatly
          when the man displayed the gloves
was that he treated the girl, whose hand he used,
          as a mere thing.
It hurt her, so that she did not even show the hurt
          but stood stiff like wood.

Always everywhere
          to treat everyone as a person
worthy and serious, and vulnerable to love

Speak with care and kindness —
          be grateful if others do.

(Even the animals they want love
like all suffering things.)

Marina is gone to Abruzzi
          for a wedding

She will be all in white
          like a small ship
trailing a veil.

Her hands will hold flowers,
she will drink wine,
                    break bread.

And she will be as beautiful
          as I have always dreamed she was.

There is the energy of a tornado in this city,
demanding bosculation, shoving, shouldering, dirt,
yet an immense beauty overflows.

Now in a roomful of flowers,
                    the window large,
out there a hillside of yellow-white and white-orange houses,
          villas, crowded squares

The sea below the city glistens like a flow of gems,
          the heaven on which the city floats.

Do we remember any compost when a flower grows?

In Naples, there's a touch of Mexico city.
That was a drabness, a flat — of dismal poverty.
Here it is all flowering and abundant, carefree,
          not in the way of degradation but of creativity.

Like an Italian domestic dessert —
                    an orange, and beside it a banana.
The orange is peeled and cut transversely,
          then laid in neat steps of slices.

The fruits can be eaten at leisure in any order.
Much better than the American "fruit salad"
          in which ten fruits mashed in little pieces
lie soused in their own juices.

Italians can also be messy — look around.

You can't judge a city or a people by the common lot
            or the popular arts — a news stand
                        like any in New York or Montreal,
and the weekend pictorials full of American stars.

E poi i turisti!

I am tired of people who come gaping at churches.
In the middle of High Mass
                        on Easter morning
they gape at the dome, while others pray with their eyes down.

Not to be with them, I will pray for this once.

The church is merely a structure
to contain the emotions of those who feel.
It is sometimes a work of art for those who do.

Italian men make their confession
        face to face with the priest, without a partition.
I do not know the history
but the first Christians must have told their sins
            out of piety and contrition,
and found this solace good.

The "shrewd psychology" of the Church
                is only the natural language of feeling.
We who never know contrition,
        or sin, or the need for oneness,
say they devised means
to inveigle or decoy the people.

But the Church is not shrewd. It is strong
because it is real : for more than a thousand years
            it was as true as poetry.

I have seen an early drawing of Jesus
                sitting on a hill, reading a book.
Beyond all the incense and sulphur
                he sits in meditation still,
a man who died for love.

And so much the memory of it is real
                that where love is, they say, he is risen.

On a church in Naples
                (inscribed over the door)
AUT PATI AUT MORI

                Better still
the liberal inscription at San Martino :
CHE IL SERVAGGIO E MALE VOLONTARIO
                                DI POPOLO
                ED E COLPA DE SERVI PIU CHE DI PADRONI.

Ah, Napoli !
Vesuvius and Somma in clouds,
the climbing streets, white and light green in the sun,
                lemon trees
(in the afternoon, fireworks for the festa),
children, tumblers of all ages,
and below, the city — a pastel white — and the bay
(any city on a mountain has beauty,
some form of action, relief — but a mountain, and a bay !)
And the Funicolare, to take you up,
and the wines . . . the cheeses . . .
the sellers of flowers, and the walls
                covered with climbing green . . .
Singing voices outside the window, a cockcrow
                every morning :
I know the world has no other city
                like Naples.
For Italy,
        it's their Aglaia —
a kind of aesthetic joy, key to their secret life.

The mistake of Montreal was to have made the mountain
a park
which nobody uses —
not even the poets, anymore,
when they might have built as in Naples
beautiful open terraces on a hill.

But even their rich homes are enclosed
pompous preserves of privacy.
They would have ruined it,
even if they had taken the chance.

And there are more beautiful houses here
than I think any architect could have devised or dreamed.
The ideas probably come like mushrooms and ferns
in a jungle.
The place is a chaos made of beautiful things.

I ragazzi !
Lighting a firecracker at the bottom of the stairs.
I watched it go off
with a piang !
And the children shrieked.
Then they played for marbles
(the great and the small).

I wonder if we would die of happiness
if we did not suffer.
Are we afraid to try ?

There are too many people. Of course there are too
many people.
But they haven't ruined the world.
They only make it more difficult to survive
(in ten years, or a hundred, we may need more men).
The point is not to stop breathing
but to make room for more.

Even the dirt is necessary.
It's some kind of beauty in ruin,
                    like a falling rose.
Even new dirt contributes to beauty,
          it is what we have to do, if we want to live.

But for any people, their life is visible
                    in the kind of beauty they create.

Architecture, sculpture —
                    correspond to the body-build.
Looking at windows, you can tell
                              the ideal Italian
                                        would be greaceful, lean.

It doesn't matter that most are short and fat.
Like a miss in darts —
          in his children, the thrower still aims.

In a way. it's one vast slum,
                    the world.
Or a rich garbage dump
on which gaudy flowers and delicate pinks
                    sprout, clamber, float ;

a ghostly beauty rising over decay

on tip-toe stems, hardly touching the earth,
          points of transparent, watery dew.

Or Mount Vesuvius smoking
          — you think it isn't beautiful ?
Or terrifying ?

Or Italian women
          — reality !
beside the Petty girls of art !

When those Hungarians
         first came to Montreal
there wasn't a place where you could sit down for a cappucino.
No wonder they started to set up restaurants.

You've got to make something out of what is there
and make it true
to that reality like nothing else, like no one else, in you.

It is no wonder the Italians love their country
         (palm trees like rocket fireworks,
               trees out of Leonardo),

and like to set up monuments,
                  and make sculptures
adding to abundance.

It is no wonder they gave life to the new Europe,
               birth to the modern.

Praise to this people,
praise even to bluff and strut
               and loud oratarical flourish.

They feel who they are, in all that poverty and dust,
               and will at least re-enact it !

But Diaz, Ethiopia . . . wars

What's the use of talking about wars ?
The war that's coming
may help us to forget any war that ever was.

(The Angel of Poetry
         must be different from any other angel
— of sex, or war

When he saw me standing there,
                    completely unemployed
he decided to come down

And this is somehow his good,
            not mine.)

A poem is like a living animal.
If you look at any poem really close
you will discover its anatomy.

Under the skin are veins, tendons, nerves
that move and hold it together.

When the girl said she hated lizards
                    at Pompei
I thought : It's all in the family, you know,
            we are all lizards.

If you loved all of it, you would also love lizards.
It's only a part of yourself you hate.

Look at your hand !

One way to solve the tourist problem
would be to admit no one without a speaking knowledge
                    of Italian —
like a graduate course in art or language.

What happens to a city
when five million people go through it in a summer ?

For one thing, the valves of hospitality may close
            — it becomes a business.

Even the walls of the museums must be worn out.

And the people, with their doors in the narrow streets,
               with their bimbi, and bags,
what have they to do with Empires,
               or art, or a Renaissance of power ?

They are the eternal soil,
               the raw matter of mankind.

To understand their little corner shrines
remember that it was Jesus
who first taught us to think of the poor and
               to love them.

The plaster is still falling
               on some of the walls of Pompei

But the lovely lizards
               are very much alive !

The past is a lost dimension.

(For relief, I used an old toilet
               once employed by the Romans.
What better
than to bring life to old ruins ?)

Unless we can see it live, it is a deep unknown —
                                        an Id
that may strangle us in our sleep.

At Pompei, the American gentleman
wanted to know whether the trees had been planted
               by the Romans.
"Who planted them ?" he asked the guard.

Beautiful letters on the wall.
(Nietzsche walked here,
and Henry James, and before that, Goethe.)

Anch' io. Canadese.

Why do we stand in awe of the past,
as if something that long ago
        must have been different, even fearful ?
We are afraid of the possible unknown !
The dead may reach out of the darkness and terrify us
with the real possibilities of the present.

For instance the ruins you can see anywhere in Naples
                (crumbling houses)
and the ruins of Pompei —
        which would we rather not see in ruin ?
And which are really best, as ruins ?
How terrible if they were still alive !
But you can buy oranges with a few twigs and leaves
                for completeness,
and lemons grow over your head as you drink coffee.
        How's that for life ?

Bella, bella. Sei bella.

Bella ragazza, bella figliuola,
                bella signorina !
(Anche bel garzone.)
Tutti bellisimi. Tutti !

Come un giardino, come una siepe
                coronata dei fiori !

Bacciamoci . . .
i belli ginocchi, labbra, occhi.

E lasciami con un grido d'amore.

The point is, no matter how great or powerful was the past,
                there is only the present,
and the past exists only as the present,
it moves us, and it is present
                because it moves us.

What we discover of the past is what we use,
                nothing else is real.

Time is the illusion
that makes all existence null and void
            and cleaves to what is living still.

So Rome is Khrushchev, America.
What was once the state is now a machine.
And the dead artists who painted walls
            are cutting flowers on Italian glass.
Nothing is lost, the world is fuller than it ever was.
What is cut down in one quarter
is probably somewhere that much more alive.
And if the whole world should perish,
do you think the powers that made us would fold up and die ?

At any rate, in Pompei, I would like to see one villa
            completely restored
according to our knowledge of how it was.

It's no compliment
to walk through the wreck of someone's home
            to peer at his household gods.

If he were living still, he would kick us out
            and clean up his midden.

I have been walking on air.
Eating delicacies and drinking coffee outdoors,
            talking of love.
While here the *lavoratore* earns
less than 800 a year
            to feed a family of ten.
And children begging point to their mouths.
And students struggle hard
to reach the status of the educated unemployed.
Too many flowers can hide a corpse !
I saw a funeral this morning
            as old-fashioned as our verse.
We've got to come to grips
with the undertow, the rocky ledge, the breaking seas.
See how destruction twists those blue Picasso limbs,
            those hands.

Look in the eyes
of the dead and dying, to close our words.

Modern Italian poetry is all elegy.
                    They know
how to celebrate defeat.
Words, either too smooth, or mangled by the teeth,
            spit in their minor verse.
And the great poets are strong with silent grief.

Addio Napoli, addio.

When a city and a poet meet —
                    isn't it like love ?
And leaving is like rending
                forever what was real.

Others will come to praise you, none more faithful,
            none more innocent —
meeting and parting in your narrow streets.

How the unreal hours pass by,
                    soon forgotten !
Where there is no ecstasy there is no reality.
That's why we slaver for the mere crust of it.

I remember the little man singing "Marutsa"
on the ship, a little red-faced Italian
with a permanent smile,
            weaving and shutting his eyes, to sing and dream :
a moment of time,
but there isn't a detail I have forgotten.

All great beauty
shows the triumph of life
            floating on a sea of storm,
a glory that must end in sighs.
At the height of great music
            (whether of Puccini or Bach)

one forgets the meaning, the lovers,
        the loss, even one's own tragedy, even God —
only to hear a sound
beyond all meaning, beyond art,
        a whiteness only, where all meanings start.

If you want a happy ending, play a tragedy backward ;
all the elements are there.
        It's just a matter of arrangement.

I believe that the poem has a generative form
            like coral or hurricane.
Every white detail must be employed.

Looking at the cold sculptures
            in the very cold museum
I saw a work of art walking about.

Her hair was brown and tumbling,
        her stockings down to her calves
                        in a tight line.

She made the place warm
        with one gleam of her smile.

Two businessmen meet in a street,
            kiss each other on the cheek
and talk.

Pork livers wrapped in bay leaves and casing
                and fried !
(Mr. Bloom would have been satisfied.)

The infinite clarity when it began
                    (if it began)

divided itself in space and time
an infinite world of infinite worlds.

Their folding together in love, and friction in pain,
unseals like mica
the leaves of quality on every hand.

Jostled in a crowded bus, in a metro —
speeding Diana —
you can feel it
(not too painful, even pleasant)
or in war, in business,
suffer destruction.

The price is suffering,
it doesn't matter.
"We've had it, Chiquita."
(The waste is frightening.)
What does matter is the dawn,
the nimbus, the brief light of love.
Try to stand in the sun for a minute once a day.

Moments of action, vigor,
flickers of life — la Beauté —
look for them in your solar calendar !

The Romans were not very imaginative.
All those gods (wall paintings of Pompei) were
a) Greek
b) invariably repeated
like so many crosses, a fixed idea.
Now they say "an archetype" but it's dead,
a decoration.
Hardly a process, a mere conception ;
and nothing is ever that true.

But an American professor told me
the Neapolitans are spineless, inefficient, thievish, vile :

dwarfish, stupid, lifeless, joyless, uncouth,
beggars, scavengers,
paupers in used clothing, ignorant,
childish, irresponsible, proud,
                              unenterprising,
avaricious, lazy, mawkish,
                    sentimental,
incontinent, over-fertile,
              and IMMORAL.

"All the men are sniffing around."

He'd have the same to say of Africa,
of India, Malaya,
          Mexico, South America, China
                    (not to speak of the Southern U.S.A.).

All the depressed areas are lacking in "spine".

But I have been in a marine aquarium and I have seen
          LOLIGO VULGARIS
          TRACHINUS ARANEUS
          SCORPAENA SCROFA
          SCYLLARIDES
          ANEMONIA SULCATA
          ASTEROIDES CALYCULARIS
          MAJA SQUINADO
          MUSTELLUS LAEVIS
          THALASSOCHELIS CARETTA
          TRIGLA CORAX
          TRYGON VIOLACEA
          HYPPOCAMPUS BREVIROSTRIS
          SPIROGRAPHIS SPALANZANII
          ACTINIA CARI
          MURAENA HELENA
          SYNGNATUS ACUS
          RETEPORA MEDITERRANEA
          PELAGIA NOCTILUCA
          PARAMURICEA CHAMALEON

Of a very graceful undulant movement
          of a pale white colour
                    with translucent fins

Fish that lie buried in the sand, on the sea bottom,
        with only their eyes peering out

Or long and thin as a pencil
                flexible in movement

Or absurd, barnacled, monstrous bulldogs of the deep,
        and sea-spiders of gigantic size.

Red flowers of the sea
                (or orange coloured)
        like carnations, like broken pieces of pomegranate

(I too was once a fish
I rubbed myself on the sea bottom, leaping gracefully
        A large fish, about two feet long)

There was one like a great sturgeon
        constantly moving and twisting its muscular body

And a fish with tentacles under the fins
        on which it walks on the sea floor !
It has a blue fin, that opens when it swims

And speckled fish, too, with the eyes of snakes
        at the bottom of the sea, their heads gently bobbing

And an Octopus
with saucer-like suckers, a paunchy body,
        huge eyes on great mounds,
blowing out of intestinal tubes,
        coiling the tips of his tentacles like a seashell.

He looked intelligent
Maybe he is intelligent, I thought, like a poet
        or a philosopher
who understands, but cannot act to circumvent clever men.

The octopus opened his magnificent umbrella,
pushed the belly forward, and bumped into a sleeping fellow

Then he went behind a pilaster
                        because I had been watching him too long.

A magnificent creature.

And I saw beautiful tiny sea-horses
                        with a fin on the back
                                    vibrating like a little wheel
And a ghostly shrimp six inches long
                        light pink and white
and graceful as a star, or the new moon

And a whorl of delicate white toothpicks
And brown stems, with white strings like Chinese
                        bean-sprouts, long and graceful.

And I saw a wonderful turtle.

But I have seen fish, turtle, octopus, with dead eyes
                        looking out at the world.
What is life doing ? waiting for something to come ?
Are we all stepping-stones to something still unknown ?
Is man, when he is glad, when he is in love or enthralled
                        at last getting a glimpse of it ?
Are the birds ? Are the swift fish ?

(Or perhaps they know they are captive. Who can tell,
even a fish may know when it is not at home.)

Then I saw a thin, thin thing
undistinguishable from a twig (just a few inches long)
but on close inspection very beautiful.

Since he has disguised himself to look so unremarkable,
                        for whom does he keep that secret form ?

There was a light green jelly
                        PHYSOPHORA HYDROSTATICA
And a kind of huge one-foot-long paramecium
                        PYROSOMA GIGANTEUM

And a thread-like plant with fragile white hair
(They say the chromosomes are such a thing of diminutive
                        size, the whole life contained in their genes !)

And a coral that was a true artistic design
                made by a growing plant —
                                a Persian decorative motif.

And many other intelligent plants, animals, and fish.

Economic empire
begins with power at the hub, administrative means,
                and "the accumulation of capital".
The periphery is there to supply and to buy.
Birmingham was not built in a day, but without the provinces
        where are the knife factories at home ?
Once the outskirts get the start (says Rostovtzeff)
                home industries fall.
Get ready for falling empires when small nations
                cease to be small.

I like the sea-bottom, says God.
Man, a creature, is limited to his natural elements.

The whole business of looking at ancient art
is to try to imagine the originals of which these
                things are copies.

The experience is very good exercise
                for an aesthetic of life.

A mother says to her children
                (crying — "There are too many of us !")
"Which of you would rather not be alive ?"

I suppose if life is too precious ever to be destroyed
it is too precious not to be brought to light.

Like poets, the truly prolific can't stop.

Of course, natural beauty can be revised ...

Ai, ai, the things that are . . .
Something there is in the things that are !

After the old beauty had been excavated and revived,
it was again subverted and cast aside —
not in the thrifts of Christianity
but in the deeper excavations of truth.

And what new easthetic
             or ideal vision is to come
out of the coil of things that are ?

Who knowns but it may be the very bread of simplicity ?

You must have wide steppes to achieve communism,
                 something easily divisible.
Where there are mountains
            and settings of natural advantage
an equalizing mood can hardly flourish.

Not that I would want it.
             God is only equal
in making much of every difference.

As for impenetrable reality, you can't beat the Romans.

I went up there
where Tiberius stood looking out at the sea.
             (It cannot have changed much.)

A vertiginous feeling.

You think you see most of Italy.
         A good view of Vesuvius —
                  the dead and the dying.

And took a shot from the top
              of the precipitous fall.
And put in fifteen cents
         for the restoration of the church.

I have a small speck of marble
                    picked up by the palace wall.
It may be the hip-bone of an ancient god,
                    or a piece of his pedestal.

Le Tre Grazie — and here is one, with a roll and a bun,
                    ambling down the Tiberian Way.
I'll make a composition of them
                    if the other two come by.

Something is making poems
as deceptively simple as ferns, fish, and pebbles.

Is the world an epic ?

Outside the window, on the square,
there was a picture
                    better than any in the room.

Of course, places that once supported a small town
cannot support a populous state.

The south was not always poor.
Every centre of empire becomes a casbah, a slum,
after the power to feed on others has failed.
Is it that the power to survive on its own labours
                    is lost — like a pampered princeling
                                cast upon the world ?
Or is there really a law of compensation ?

How lucid the Frenchman was
                    explaining the problems of Italy,
how precise in phrase :
Much money in a few hands... in the south...
poverty, people without sustenance...
Commerce difficult... credit buying a common fraud
(appliances bought for credit and sold for quick cash).

How well he put it, about the effort to reduce
                sales, to "improve the quality of trade".

But the Cartesian virtues cannot help, they cannot diminish
suffering, of soften the hard content of reality.

It's harrowing to see the poor.
"You gave her too much," said the man.
"They won't respect you for it."

What shall I do ?
Go back to America and live on $10,000 a year
        (six and a quarter million lire),
with meat and pie, thick cream and coffee,
                and cartonfuls from the A & P
for the weekend, or any week day

And forget . . . and write poems . . . and be happy
(A man here earns 850 dollars a year).

I look at a streetful of blue exhaust,
a wet trail on the sidewalk where someone pissed
                in the early hours,
or a man with a burlap bag,

since cities are all the same with their modern baggage —
vast accumulations of beaten, bedraggled mankind.

Only the Emperor's men are happy, with knives in their backs,
handing out corn to the people.

The modern world is hungry for gladiators, for ravenous beasts
        fierce with frustration like themselves.

The street rocks with *scavamenti* and gas-smells.

In one of the tapestries of the Sec. XVI
it amused me to see cattle
                quietly chewing grass

while near them, over a little stream,
men were butchering one another, in furious battle.

I believe the classical art never ended.
There are thirteenth century nudes
                    carved on a pedestal
that have the shapely beauty of Greek gods.

And in a Botticelli Madonna,
            how the Neo-Platonic essence is still conveyed !
Beauty without desire.

The eyes of realists are lifted up in contemplation.
A delicacy of line. Translucent veils, and gold.

But the slaughter of the Innocents ?
What does that nightmare mean ?

To judge from Caravaggio
the Italians were always a hysterical people
            (*Crisi* . . . three times in a page of news)
Everything here seems fit to explode.

Maybe things have come to that pass.

In Titian's Danae for instance, the gold
                is coming down in minted coins.
Fucked by money . . .
            There's an archetype for you.

Truth, truth ! (those aristocrats and kings
            who let themselves to be painted by Goya) . . .
Yet drama becomes melodrama ;
religion, love, beauty
            become sentimental sop.

(Not to meddle with the history of decadence,
        stay in the centre with the strong.)

Western art comes down from myth to actuality,
        and always lies when it prettifies.
Which is more real, the myth or the reality ?
Neither. Reality is a truth that is possible to both.

On the nineteenth century I close my book.
Art had gone so far wrong
        it made even the artists sick.

And democracy as a mere leveller
        swept away a lot of decadent rubbish,
but it does not define the good.

In a strange place,
once the strange becomes familiar, one feels out of place ;
because the newly familiar is still not quite familiar,
the really familiar is some other place.

How sad for those without a home !

(No one has suffered more in our time
        than refugees, exiles, cut off from home.)
And yet everyone, everywhere, always, is cut off from home.
Everyone, even at home, feels somehow not quite at home.

Actually, I've never liked Plato (any more than travel)
        and wouldn't versify his prose.

Change is all we ever know, not bullion.
But all that great change is nothing still.

What is it moves ? Since it is true — *E pur si muove !*

Rome doesn't know, and Plato never knew.

Here's the beginning, with Galileo, a new ignorance
— is what I want to say.

We fractured beings
— that we should love one another !
must bring joy to the unity that made us one.

Yet I saw hatchets, swords, pistols, armour, spears,
in a great museum,
any one of which must have killed many men.

And looked at the edges of swords that had rent flesh,
and at guns, hung out for display.

Is there less love in us than will to destroy ?

They say : *che solo uomo assomiglia a Dio.*

A shoemaker down the street talked to me for about an hour
(sitting in his dark shop, on a low chair, on a cement floor
holding a plastic globe, studying the world)

and he said —
about poverty, about peace, about killing, about war —

Let the powers get together and say
What kind of world do we want ?
Do we want to destroy the world ?
Or do we want to make it better ?
Then join forces to improve our life !

How can the working man live on twelve hundred lire a day
(less than $2 in USA
And what do rich people want with all their money ?
Everything comes from the soil, from the tiller of the soil !
Let them rent land for a share of the produce,
or let them help the people on the land !

(He spoke in Italian,
lifted out of himself like an actor by an authentic role.

After all, who are the best communists ? The Americans !
They want no classes, no inequalities —
                    Why do they quarrel with the Russians ?

If the Russians do better
            — why deny it, why oppose ?
Why not praise and imitate whatever there is to praise ?

As for people, the Italians are a good people
                            (*buono popolo*)
though they like riot, and noise.
Why fire bullets into crowds of people
as they have done it, in Hungary, in Czechoslovakia ?

        Why not let the people live ?

Brother (he called me *fratello*),
                Italy is the garden of Europe :
we send out oranges, lemons, olives, grapes,
                                to all the world

and our own people have nothing left to eat.

The trouble with most lives is too much sameness.
And the trouble with travel is too much difference.
'The real world' is only
                what we're most accustomed to.
But the real is something else — to be found
as much in fixity as in change.

No matter how it glitters, how it shines,
                            it will vanish.
The street vendors, the Partenope, the trees
                will vanish.
The pink and lemon walls, the grey, the dark designs
will fade like chalk in a pale snowy light
            and leave only memory, tracings in a dream.
And we will discover other cities with the same
                beauty, looking for the one true
and lasting city, that may never be.

2

Two Italian honeymooners, from Firenze,
                              on the way to Capri.
O how one wishes them well !

Speak of joy, sunshine, beauty ...
Everything, everywhere, shall be well.
All things for them shall be well.

How pleasant it is to be always on the way,
                    to be in motion,
to see new rivers, plains,
to talk to new people from far places,
                    to discover even the musty past.
How pleasant, to be carried like a seed in a stream.
To see the sediments out of which new life may come.

If lovers do not read poetry
                    how can they love ?
How can their desires be shaped in the form of a dream ?

In travel, as on any visit,
          it is important not to overstay.
Extreme illusions
are vivid only for a day — the real
                    illusions are the most unreal.

Leaving Naples, for some reason
          Handel's *Amen* was singing in my ears.
Poesie : *Esercizi spirituali.*

Italian suburbs look like the ruins of Pompei.
Then the beautiful autostrada,
                    and orchards
to take the traveler away ...

from divisions, here where a city is still a nation
(and "Napoletani" means something racial,
                    like "the Irish" or "Mexicanos").

How is it some are more advanced ?
Canadians are retarded at the frontier,
                as Italy is retarded in the past.
The present is a kind of life
            in which new objects teach us how to think,
and buildings, business, schools, and jet planes are
                context scenery for the new imaginings of art.

But only those at the center feel
the pressures and thrusts that make imagination real.

There is incredible mountain landscape
                between Naples and Rome,
cultivated fertile valleys,
vineyards, neat green fields, delicate trees.

But this has all been done, it has been used.

The red earth of Italy, red earth,
anywhere that men have lived long.

And the prosperity of the north
                        which is excellent land,
a beauty and fertility almost unbelievable.
(Like the heart's soil, that lies fallow, unused,
                in our disordered lives.)

Erasmian fields, Mozartean streams.

I saw people living in an arch of an aqueduct
            built by the Romans ...

But great old cities
             never lose their loud resounding tone
and sometimes build on it.

I am glad to be back in modern Rome —
Here on the Via Veneto is the Canadian Pacific
                    Airlines
                    Steamships
                    Railways
I'm a city-dweller
The sounds, the shops, the streets are all familiar
             fictions, like Coke and home.

Like a lot of crazy crickets, the students
             on the Festa della Matricola
walk, ride, block the streets, blowing whistles.
One of those things you simply *can't miss* —
             it's a pain in the ears !

In Rome, where the cities are heaped on one another,
the new most powerful,
             shouldering away the past,
yet unwilling, or unable, to erase those monuments,
time makes it an accumulation of glorious rubbish
             that once was real
                    as the violent traffic on the square.

Weak is Hadrian now, less than a shadow,
                    whose column was once new.
Pitiful the dead, who made much of power
                    in the world they ruled.
Even a child may laugh at Caesar, or ignore him going by ;
though lumps of stone, patched with brick, show
             how real they thought they were.

If they could only speak, I'm sure they'd tell us —
             "Sweep away
                    these triumphs, ruins
                           of our 'glorious day'.

SENATVSPOPVLVSQVEROMANVS
INCENDIOCONSVMPTVMRESTITVIT

Only for the living, the past lives ;
by the Capitol, I remembered
the place where we got a bottle of coffee
                and took it out to the car . . .

The dead, if they share with us
                        whatever they loved,
are dear as the sun.

Keats died in a little house by the Spanish Stairs
                near S. Trinita dei Monti.
Something of him still lives, in the brown stone,
                        in the plain windows,
simple and clean, and sad like his poems — permanent
though he came here only to die.

(Ah, there is so much of our past
                        everywhere in this city
that I can hardly believe there is such a thing as time.)

When the builder put up those stones, did he say —
"You've got to stand until a poet comes
                        to make you speak !"

Anyhow, this shows we're not to make too much of anything.

In the midst of the Forum, on a white stone,
                I sit, like a bird trying to hatch an egg.
I contemplate the ruin like art,
                        though it isn't art.
It is the ruin of life (which is like art)
                or what we often get from art.

Strong as life, the features of death
                seem to whisper about extinction,
and ask us what we are, were, or would be.

When the busses pass here, the ruins shake so
            it's a wonder they don't tumble down.
Some are certainly persistent
            even when they are dead and gone.

I think of what this city looked like when it was new
(even as a broken skull
            may help one imagine the shape of a man).

It's hard to believe
that all this has been here for two thousand years ...
And will probably last another two thousand.

Oh, we would like to make some things endure !

The modern bus (on which I mount) passes
                        by the old Colosseum —
black hulk of a dead dinosaur lying in the middle of the city
Efficient, actual, the present moment
                        is cleaned up for action,
as if it were all that will ever exist.

In the Villa Borghese gardens, high and beautiful trees
            seem to vanish into the blue.
The sun sits like a bird
            somewhere in those branches.

I believe the purpose of all being
is to be luminous and reaching like these trees —
true to the character of beauty
            that moves and is whatever moves.

But like the discarded shell of a living crustacean
            (living because we are living)
the ruins stand — refuse to be cleared away ;
though cleaned up by clever scavengers
who reconstruct what is forever beyond recall —
a primitive unconscious
to the living Romans and the Embassy of the U.S.A.

I thought I saw you, Aglaia,
          walking down the street, in a green dress —
your slim legs vanished in the crowd.

I knew you, from a kind of after-joy.

As much as to say that what we are looking for
          is always there before us.

Every energy is an angel.
But there is a great deal of waste in nature.
Man is perhaps an attempt at economy.

God (that word) like a great gambler throws the dice of things
and gathers only when the fall succeeds ;
but man would load the bones with love.

The sunlight on the tree across the street
          seems a crimson sprinkling of luminous blossoms.
Deeper among the trees a rose light fills the park,
          making the tree trunks soft and pliable ;
yet above them the dark greenery floats
          alive with the whistling of a million swallows.

We should all write like John Keats, about to die,
          leaving the poem fragrant on the air
like the evening hour, that is its own good reason for being.

Studious young men were walking among the ruins
          with notebooks, writing things down.
Are they all writing this poem ? I think they are.

"We are not capable of pleasant sexless relations."

ETIAM NOBIS BREVIS ET PERITURA VOLUPTAS
QUA PETIMUS TRISTI MIXTA DOLORE NOCET

Looking at Cranach's Venus, I saw in front of me
              a girl's flea-bitten neck.

Ah, Botticelli ! You were right at the first !
Beauty is real, even if those who make it are not !

What does that slander mean ?

They have selected eidolons, which we know are real,
and made them the objects of touch and desire.
But what are eidolons, that they are better than joy or pain ?
Made of shadows, are they more real than shadows ?

Like those trees, that shed lights of meaning
              to stop the flicker of time,
art is sealed in happiness, happiness is pure art.

Every joy is a timeless moment,
              pain (and death) only its price.

All this is pragmatic !
              Not that we want to know
but that we want to live !

In the dark corridor yesterday, I hit my head against a wall.
Isn't that a sign ?

Aglaia ! in the Italian sun ... Blinding.

No city's so big that you can't make a perambulation of it
              in a few hours.
I have walked now in every part of Rome,

and I have seen ...
              (looking at wall paintings done about the year 700)
the face of God, as they saw him
              and the saints SCS. IOANNIS, etc.

(the world's a shaky thing)

a right-angled Christ
              (not so much suffering as patient)

and the holy men still gazing from the walls.

I seem to peer through time, as through a tottering mansion,
to glimpse the shapes beyond, the spectral bone-men
who lived, and died, and believed.

And see the new religion fearfully replacing the old,
burning temples,
knowing, past cure, how sure their reasons were
against the old idols,
who now are burned themselves, with the sure fire of reason.

Nothing stands, we say, we moderns.
All's flux, an art of mathematics — of fiery matter,
while the old gods gutter and die in the flames.

Yet it's something one wouldn't know without coming —
that ruins are peaceful
(white stone, and the smell of clover)

Not that it is the past, it isn't really
— just fragments, that no one wants to use

like nature (TO PAN), where nothing practical ever happens
(no buying and selling)
so only quiet people come, to sit and ruminate.

"Le trèfle, l'avoine et l'herbe des champs..."

The limitations of practicality !
Said the English lady :
"*Uova,* an egg !
Why don't they say *egg* and have done with it ?"
All these foreign languages ! ...
"I don't see why people can't speak English
and make themselves understood."

Even if ours is the best, there may be others.

As the Greek said to the sailors :
"Now which of you is the god ?"

Azalias at S. Trinita dei Monti
          bloom the year long —
as permanent as one could desire.

But at the park on the Pincio
          many noses were broken
on the faces of heroes (something that could not have happened
          in ancient Rome),
even Dante, defaced.

To overthrow an empire, the vandals are always with us.

Lousy with anti-semitism, in reverse,
          the anti-Christian hater also destroys.

And yet with rare sense of humour
the Catholics have placed a shrouded, over-draped figure
          (some funerary female)
before the naked Venus of the Capitoline museum.

The Church never gives up !

And the Esquiline Venus, divine first of sexual energy,
          says, "Find me !"

Should we climb the ladder of love till we are famished ?
          Are not the common loves good enough ?
Where would the world be if there were only gods ?
Let every faulty detail be enjoyed !

If Cardinal Newman had gone a little further back
          he might have ended a Jew.
Christians have always feared heresy because they are
          themselves a heresy.
But that's no reason to hate Christians —
          though it may be a point for the Jews.

Once of course the Church militant had teeth of stone.
You can tell from the Pantheon
most of those buildings would still be standing
if it weren't for the Church of Rome.

I visited the Campo de' Fiori
                where I stayed with you then
(in the Albergo del Sole — it still stands)
And looked at Giordano Bruno, who burned on that square :
                QUI
          OVE IL ROGO ARSE
                    (where the bonfire burned)

And now, a city like that —
                not permitted to die —
but dragging the past with it into the present —
What a burden !
It is perhaps by good fortune that they destroyed each other,
                as they always do,
else where would we be, if all that bric-a-brac still existed ?

(And had tea in front of the old church
                and watched the pretty girls passing.)

The Italians must be religious, else they would become
                little dogs.
I watch the young men pick up the girls . . .

It must be religion that makes them refuse !
Else they would be all day in one another's arms . . .

At night on the Via Crispi
the prostitutes, one with the face of a plaster wall,
one like a small tight inflated doll,
                offer it for 10,000 lire
in the Via della Purificazione.

The sacred can be destroyed, Aphrodite
                and the chaste temples of Apollo
were brought to the ground, in the savage Christian wars.

And yet there is no shortage of churches.

Michaelangelo's Pieta will stand
                until a new religion comes

to destroy that great quiet.

But one doubts, whether any can,
whether anything like that will ever again be sacred.

Darling, sd. the Italian,
              you are refreshing as Coca-Cola !
La Dolce Vita comes (the unreal life)

Not even the voice of Di Stefano, Tebaldi
                    in the choruses of Puccini . . .
no ecstasies to come !

And the tragic face of Mussolini
              in the second-hand bookstalls.
Tragic, the soul of Italy
pours out in melodrama, in pathos,
                    unable to contain it
(like Michaelangelo become Bernini)
The broken dream of an operatic greatness
shattered by gunsmoke, suicide, car-gas, rock-&-roll
and the barbiturates of tourism . . .
              Now a face on the bookstalls
                    in the botteghe oscure,
chin jutting out, clean-shaven, with the steady eye
recalling a twenty-five year triumph
              ending without an encore.

They should not have hung him up by the heels.

It's the unreal life I would discase of,
              kick the death's head off
and meet the world . . .

I saw a young man this morning,
              erect, handsome,
with a face of withheld suffering,
because a small purple patch on his cheek
had begun, that would cover his face.

One life is given us — to be spoiled by a verruca !

I'd rather laugh, sitting in my coffin . . .
Stand up and laugh, the bones breaking, feet numb,
than look at the *pigra vita*
      (that we know too well) — and look at the sun !

Not for a skin disease, but a flower
      of the unspoiled face no one sees.

The modern arts have discovered chaos,
      they have not discovered the gods.
They have discovered only the roar of titanic powers.

The gods, whatever they are, exist
      before men can begin to exist.
We are living on the castoff shards of the former gods.

On my last day in Rome, instead of a tour of the ruins,
I went to visit the zoo.

A change of scene.

Monkeys, giraffes, pumas, hippos, a leopard, kangaroos
      (one riding in the pouch of its mother —
          how they leap, and how they crawl),
eagles and swans, tigers and elephant seals ;
monkeys (I thought
the monkey resembles a dog as much as it does a man)
and the orang-utang (an ugly creature
      to be related to someone as beautiful as you).

If we are ugly, for all that
the Greeks imagined a human beauty.

The real life, of the birds, the beasts, the swift cheetah
(it was a very comfortable zoo
      with lots of space for the animals . . .)
The beauty of the African lion among the high rocks
(I waved to him, he turned away his head)
Tiny nibbling deer (gazelles) and elephants
      moving their huge trunks with ease
Zebras, with perfect stripes, and camels complete with humps.

Every detail perfect as on the day of creation
                    (which is now)
and all the records, as on the monumental horse, complete.
Even the rhinoceros, and the hippopotamus —
                              all the past revealed !

The zoo is man's full nature displayed in detail :
sloth, vigour, zest, appetite, cruelty, dirt and lust ;
as well as neatness, delicacy and care,
                    ineffable grace —
even wisdom, even grandeur ;

and the look of suffering ;

but also beauty, function, a difficult adjustment
that makes of living a triumph and an art.

In coats of many colors, the birds
the infinite families of beasts, of fishes —
                              extinction is not a loss,
in the present it is all complete,
                    all that it ever was.

Volturina, the peacock,

                    Flamingoes, Cranes — *Gru !*

          Arcopiteco, Lemures,

Mandrillo,   *Mangabe,*   *Gelada*

          Giaguaro,   *Pinguino, Oca,*

                    Cereopside, Moretta,

Testugine, Pitone, Stambocco,

          Tapiro, Orso, Cigogna, Alce, Aquila

Yet somehow best of all, the human families
          elders walking about explaining to the young

Two lovers, sitting beside me, hiding from a brief rain ;
          soldiers, awkward, on a day's leave ;

an officer with his wife and father and little son ;
            two friends walking arm in arm,
a group of little children, with a nurse ; two boys
                    romping around ;
nuns, old people, sons and fathers, children —
            all who come to see the living world,
and feel the whole creation for it more alive.

We should import from Africa
        bananas, fine wood, hides,
        sugar, cotton, thread,
        rope, ivory, nuts, coffee, and exotic grains.
From Italy, wines, oranges, lemons,
        cheeses, sculptures (let them be copies),
        music, minestrone, and the art of love.

All we are looking for, so distant,
            so difficult, so near ...
in each, the least, the same, chaos and blind chance
        —out of which nothing, or something,
            or some great good may come.

The gods are not behind it all, they are in front of it.
They do not make things happen.
        They find it enough to approve.

Yet Rome's rickety monuments —
            a wonder they do not fall down and kill
the living, in envy, for some of the things we do.

I went to see one of the gods
                    still living
Ezra Pound
            by the Domus Aurea
in Rome, in the city of Propertius,
            of Marcus Valerius Martial

the greatest river god of them all

dying, in a great bed, into immortality
                    like those other ruins
(yet thin, and beautiful as youth)
that once were pillared in marble form
                    by the sacred wood of arches

And he said ...
                    well, nothing
Only the tears filled his eyes
                    as the great heart beat badly

And I walked around that place a little, and went my way.

Then I was sitting in the park having my cheese and bread
when two boys came clamoring like crows :
                                    "Fa--me ! Fa--me !"
wanting food.

I gave them money, and gave them some bread and cheese.
                    They ate ravenously, like thieves.

EXTINCTORI TIRANNORVM
AC PVBLICAE SECVRITA —
        AVCTORI

It was by the house of Nero.
After a long time, nobody cares what harm he did.
They want his records.

But Ezra has never done harm.
            He has never done anyone harm.
See his records.

If I stayed in Rome any longer
            I would not see any more ruins,
I would try to live. Get work somewhere, teaching
                    (English, or modern lit.)
and make a place for myself among the others.
I'd soon forget about the past
            — except as it ticks in our own marrow.

I said : I will take the train now, and meet a student girl
            who will talk to me about the schools.

I did ! She was very beautiful.
(Her name was Maria-Teresa, from Terni.)

3

Well, I no longer visit churches
but every day walk up and down the aisle
                        of Santa Maria Novella.

In Florence, where I saw Dante explain his book,
and the stone where he sat
                        at evening
(a piece of marble set in a wall
        between a tailor shop and a store for religious trinkets),
and some frescoes that Vasari ruined, painting them over.

I walked three circles around the spot where Savonarola died,
and bowed before the houses of great men,
                Michelangelo, Dante, Alfieri
                        (extending the metaphor over a day)
and walked home through the narrow streets
            in a kind of stupor or trance.

While in Paris a crisis had been averted,
        tanks and troops removed from the streets ;
a revolution in Cuba quelled,
                    order restored,
with the promise of force, or war, to keep the peace.

In Laos the people are lashing each other with shrapnel.
Surely the fell determination of small nations is at hand,
surely the division of empires is at hand.

I sit on a stone like Dante
      and ruminate about the realms.
"Peace has been restored," as in Michelangelo's day,
         with time for a few uncompleted sculptures.

The banging of the bells in the square,
the cumulus clouds, over the tower,
and the bright sun blinding the eyes ;
this is what Dante meant, about the sun,
            and Milton speaking of light —
like bits of glass
in a cathedral wall shivering the sight.

As if somewhere, high there, that church, or city, stood
that every fragment of the good remakes, restores
         to temporary sight.

We must learn to look at modern art
            as we look at the past,
with a nodding glance at the hundreds of minor pictures,
but understanding, and admiration, for the few.

In Fra Lippo Lippi's Madonna
you will see it is more than just a picture of his mistress
            (the woman a man loves) ;
more chaste than any wife, or many a widow —
            or one of your tactless virgins
reading the comic books and Hollywood news.

In any case, a beauty
         not for any man's praise or blame.

Did we become real —
         and then too real ?
Or did we misuse the real, and lose it,
            in the apparent real ?
From Giotto to Titian ...
(Obscene women are not real
      — the 'slave girls' of Victorian sculpture —

yet the Danae of Titian, or Venus of Botticelli, are.)
Even Brueghel, Cranach, Dürer
                        are still "real".
But not Salvator Rosa, running away from — what ?
Since Italy never reached the realism of the Germans
            (unless it was in Leonardo's cartoons) —
                        the hells of Brueghel of the Inferni,
                                the tortures of Hieronymus Bosch,
                                or Dürer's Melancholy.
You must first go down, into the real, and then come up.

Look at Taddeo Zucchini, The Assumption —
the Virgin in an odd, backward-leaning pose
Tiny cherubs appear in light, in holes in the clouds
Others, fully painted,
                        are elongated, shapely nudes
The Angels playing instruments, harp, lute, and viol
There is a blue landscape in the distance
And down below, on earth,
            behind the flower-strewn bed of rushes
                                from which she rose,
a grim altar, with death's head, cross, holy book,
            and hour-glass — all that she has left behind.

Or see — "Orson Welles on a Tortoise"
                (the fountain in the Pitti courtyard),
postcard 20 cents.

I passed the house where Shelley wrote 'The West Wind'.

In the Annunciation of Martini and Memmi,
the Angel's AVE GRATIA PLENA DOMINUS TECUM
is written in gold, on gold —
                        an almost inaudible whisper.

Angels leave only strips of cloud.

But the lady said, "Artists are not concerned with subject
                                            matter at all."

I suppose that thought is inhibited in us moderns
                    like the "sex" of Freud,
we don't want to think
about lost beauty, or nobility, or love, or belief,
nor even of the possibility of these things.

So we say 'The content does not concern an artist'
            or 'He is not concerned with subject matter at all.'

There is the vacuum at the end of things,
before the hurricanes begin.

In the early times,
all that we know of many a painter
is that he left his work in a certain chapel or church.

With the decadence (the 16th century)
"The Massacre of the Innocents" became a popular subject.
Painters, still later, excelled in "Battles" and "Butcherings".
And they signed these things.

E allora . . .

    Italia, where boys in the streets make collections "for those
                                            in prison",
and the barber shops are open on Sunday,
and there are exhibits of children's art in the underground.

Students in crowds, shouting and singing, go down on
                                            their knees
in the square of the Signoria
        before the statue of Freedom, in Florence.
Flowers overflow the Portico and the Piazza.
The orators speak for the working people
                    by a fountain full of coins.

Domestic art
was the mode of the nineteenth century,

yet life and art are always being renewed.
the new clean wide streets,
　　　　business buildings, shopping areas, apartments ;
the new art, of energy and expression,
　　　　　　an infinite profusion of new forms...
The world is never at an end.
As soon as one thing's finished another is ready to begin.

Young people with guitars and colored hats take pictures,
crowds in the streets are singing.

The crooked streets, the yellow zig-zag heaps of houses,
the chatter of the people, and the sound of clamor indoors,
the quick vitality of the women, making love to the men :
the white clouds, and the afternoon crowds
walking, talking, or drinking apéritifs in the cafés.
A musician among his friends
　　　　singing *Vesti la giubba* from a chair,
or the common humanity of not-so-pretty girls
　　　　　　　　with their boy-friends,
or husbands with their wives, and a thermos, and a bag
　　　　　　of oranges and a lunch,
going to see the town.
Old men leaning on canes, nodding,
boys in trim knee-pants.
I hear a man in Italian say to his daughter :
"We'll have something to eat, and then a cake"
　　　　　　—she wanted so much to buy the sweet !
And someone shouts, "Cameriere ! un po' di buon vino !"
　　　　　(family people ... or lovers ...)
to the ringing, on the square, of iron gongs.

Later accordions in the street, playing for money
　　　　　(this kind of thing in Florence is not begging,
　　　　　　　it's useful work, and well paid).

I walk by the Arno, *in sul passo d'Arno,*
　　　　　　　and watch the fishing boys.
In the bushes by the water lovers sink into each other's arms
　　　　　(it's Sunday),
the sun sets over the distant hills and towers...

The pointilist poem ends
        in praise of common things
in Dante's city, of Leonardo's dream,
        where Manzoni improved his speech :
and now people come, from thirty kilometers off, on a Sunday
to walk by the Arno and move in the crowded streets.

Art became democratic by the nineteenth century
        and therefore trivial,
because the common, whatever already exists,
is never equal to the good we can imagine.

In disgust with common things, artists were driven to satire
so far did the reality fall below their need.

Ideal .... but the Ideal must be real, not a sop

(unless you have some great good in your life
        you will have nothing at all to say).

The days, the streets, the people,
        are an unstable means, a bridge
to what is yet to be, or else can never be entire—

that grows, and moves, like clouds
        piling over the world and time,
in the cloud-white of marble
        or an acropolis of words.

Certainly this cross-section of an instant
        is not all the world there is.

Sitting before the Eternal Church I write with my ephemer
        hand
"What makes you think you are eternal ?"
And yet the Church pretends to what I most desire.

The people had built pyramids, walls, aqueducts,
and dragged stones, had their bodies crushed under stone,
                    state, and taxes enough,
to deserve "suffering" as the word, above all,
            in sermons, in art, in books, for two thousand years.
They had suffered so that it had been almost two millenia
before they could join their suffering with a little joy.

As for "master morality",
            that was always possible for the masters.
Unless like Shaw we foist a "master morality" on the poor ;
they don't want it, don't need it—
            the vengeance-morality of the mob.
Any true morality wants justice for the slaves,
those who have been crushed by the masters in their
                                centuries of pride.

(People who prepare your lunch for you
            are of course concerned with "simple utility".
Why despise them for it ?)

As for Plato, if the universe of ideas is complete
I do not see the point of its continuing to plague us
            in this transitory way.

It is what becomes real that contains the ideas,
and all things are a part of whatever it is becomes.

Though the "old town" we find so picturesque is a slum
with its narrow crooked streets and drains
            (think of the old city downtown, back home).

Modern Florentines live in the suburbs,
            in villas along the Arno ;
while this quaint mess is a kind of museum of antiquities,
and in the middle of the lot you have the tourist shops.

Beauty without utility becomes slick.
On the other hand
at the International Exhibition of Arts and Crafts

Jugoslavia exhibited four cases of ammunition
                          from their armament works.

The Canada Exhibit consisted of Indian moccasins,
                    parkas, Eskimo ware, blankets
and a few odd pieces of ceramic.

(A very primitive polar country.)

But I have loved the old churches,
          the quiet of Santa Maria Novella (off season),
the dark shadows, the arches and illuminated windows,
and stood before the Venus of Titian
                    and the paintings of Botticelli
(seeing his face in one of the canvasses, hardly believing)
and walked about so stirred that ordinary things
became foreign to me, and I asked—
what we are in comparison with that vision,
          and whether we are real, or if not, what is real ?

Because great art touches something stronger and more
                                            compelling
than anything in life we touch or see.

And yet we say it is only "from imagination" ;
the ordinary trivial things,
          whether we want them or not, do really exist—
while the reality of art we say does not exist.

"As if what we imagined were more real than what we know !"

But it is so. What we imagine is more complete and perfect
          than anything in the world of change.
For if the mind is real and more than a lifeless object,
then what the mind desires is at the heart of nature ;
it is what the world means (rather than what it seems to be) —
at least as a supreme guess, out of our ignorance,
          that tells us we might yet succeed.

64

All the way from Parma to Milan
the Italian students were discussing the uses of prayer

with the subtle music of gay young voices
en route to take an examination in the schools.

Ach, what a long voyage !

II

"Il suffit de marcher sur les bords de la Seine pour recevoir de la terre une force heureuse qui permet d'exprimer tous les dons."

MARCEL PAGNOL

1

One must cross mountains, going from one world to another.
Skirting the Alps, we saw jagged peaks
      hang down as if the earth were newly torn,
and glaciers like frozen lightning against the sky.

There were white peaks
hurtling hard against the cumulus, and torrents
coming down on heaps of moraine.

As reality
is torn by bombs, and threats, and civil war,
the mountains seem to groan under a new-old fury
prophetic always of things to come.

Pressure of the suns
      buckles the atoms together,
but man is a later structure
            who undoes the work of the sun.

With a spark of the fire that burns in the stars
smoldering in our ashes,
we plan to try another earth, or finish this one.

Vevey, city of my other self, Rousseau...

Could he conceive a savage in outer space?
And wouldn't he ask as we do — what is real?

[The First American came back with, "Boy, what a ride!"
And Gagarin: "Please tell the Government, the Party, etc..."]

Dreams!... Think of the real ghosts we knew!
Something in the oval of that face
           survives her dream.

When I spoke to the two Frenchmen on the train
          about French Canada,
they said they hadn't given it much thought.
You have a vested interest in us, I said,
      realer than Algeria, and politically as good.

Looking at my watch, I think of my wife and child :
    "He is in bed," or "Now they are asleep."
Even the actual, if it is alien to us, seems unreal.

All travel is like fiction,
    visiting foreign lands, antique and new,
that the inhabitants call real.
And always when one at last perceives this,
    seeing the hum-drum beneath the illusion,
one must leave. There is no point
    in being caught in other people's fictions.

After awhile, of course, the world runs out of novelties
    with which to amuse us.
We must fall back on the truth
that all things are only new and strange
    because they are ephemeral.

What is it that a poet knows
    that tells him — 'this is real' ?

Some revelation, a gift of sight,
granted through an effort of the mind —
    of infinite delight.

All the time I have been writing on the very edge of knowledge,
heard the real world whispering
    with an indistinct and liquid rustling —
as if to free, at last, an inextricable meaning !
Sought for words simpler, smoother, more clean than any,
    only to clear the air
of an unnecessary obstruction ...

Not because I wanted to meddle with the unknown
    (I do not believe for a moment that it can be done),
but because the visible world seemed to be waiting,
    as it always is,
somehow, to be revealed.

Whoever has once heard that music, in that quiet light,
knows what he has to say, over again and over.

Even the Iron Curtain is full of holes.
                    In this hotel in Paris
large groups of tourists from Soviet Russia
make their stay — ordinary people (like you and me)
who gesture at table, love laughter, and play accordions
                    in their rooms :
on a tour of Paris, Côte d'Azur, Rome.
"Ils sont bien surveillés," said the waitress.
But one can break through. Controls are never that complete.

Nature is actually an open secret,
we can try to read it.

Jak to pszyjemnie swój własny język usłyszeć!

My true tongue.
No, only another language,
                    of childhood.

Intellect, which is the glory of France,
            l'esprit géométrique
                        refines
taste to a daintiness in action,
                jewellery of words,
delicate cookery, pâtés, small cakes
(they have brought the croissant to perfection)
and assorted cheeses
(Are the ingredients lacking in America
        that Kraft cannot improve their process ?)
A fine exfoliation of ideas, like Gide's or Proust's,
releases the kept odours of the rose.

Intellect some Frenchman said — or mathematics —
            is the language of God.

The French, who have done more than any other people
            to keep the Index alive,
go on writing books, after they've had Voltaire,
        Villon, Stendhal, Flaubert, Anatole France,
            Gide and Proust.

71

They want to be the only nation
                that writes books.

Stores and counters on every corner,
          books for a quarter or a dime.
Mountains of nonsense, poetry, history — and the latest
                          greatest prose
What a pleasure it is to be among a people
          who have learned to read !
What a destruction of the settled mind !
No wonder they threaten their best authors with murder.
Great ideas, here, have become so unspecialized
          that ordinary people turn them into prose,
overthrow the law ... curse life ...
                defame the very sperm
(then hang like guts in a butcher's stall).

And they want to go further — further with annihilation —
          when there is no further to go !
(Don't worry, however, the French will find a way.)

How was the god contained in a picture or a sculpture ?
Was he not real ?
When the great Phidias shaped her form
Aphrodite came down like the Word
          and became marble, and dwelt among us.
And when the Lucchese artist painted Christ
                with his terrible sure hand
he fixed the reality, a bent body, forever on a cross —
          nailed it, nailed it.

Are we blind that we cannot see ?

As for madness,
          if the gods were to speak to us only in madness
we would not need the gods.

Because then men would be superior to the gods.

But the gods are not the voices of madness,
          they are of light, and they are intelligences.

Mens sana : not slavery.

But there are all kinds on the newsstand :
                              La Vie des Bêtes
                                 La Vie au Soleil
                    La Vie Française
                                          FEMME
                    La Vie Parisienne
                    NUS

It's the character of the women,
                      like no other city,
mobile, fanciful, swift,
            enduring with spirit, with chic
(only French girls know how to make a moue,
            only Parisiennes tell you with their hands).
I've watched a working girl in a white frock
                      swinging a basket
and a great fat woman between the tables, selling meat,
and "Tropical Fish" with long gloves
                              on the rue de l'Opéra
(there's one shouting now, selling the news,
an actress, at her stall, bringing the house down with
                                          applause ...)

Yet in the street I saw a woman slap a child,
            and heard him cry out.
Blood rushed to my face and I wanted to shout —
                      "Ne faites pas ça ! ..."

A child like my own, a little boy crying.
It seems to me if we only loved some one thing enough
            we couldn't be cruel to any other.

On a Sunday morning
I like to go to some great old church to attend Mass.
Actually, just stand on the bare stone and maybe write a poem.

The people, who take it more simply,
                    kneel at the first remove
from whatever it is emotion and symbol mean.

We lean in a shadowy world when the organ peals
                    like a slain bull
and the great windows bleed.

Go out in the sun,
the shops are open, and the cafés clink :
                    feel the chill breeze
frisk the untrammeled world of small coins.

Although sermons pretend
to squeeze the last drop of feeling
                    from a literal, sentimental story . . .

I don't know what the church can do.

Perhaps read the signs
                    only as signs,
to teach the people truth.

(Je ne suis pas croyant,
                    mais je crois à la vérité
que la croyance toutefois recherchait.)

In St. Séverin the interior was being cleaned,
                    half-finished :
the ancient dark aisles and arches,
                    and the newly-clean section
as it must have looked when it was first built,
                    side by side.

A kind of loss,
since part of the beauty of old buildings is their age,
which appears in the ruined corners —
                    the dark erosions of time.

Why is the old beautiful merely in being old ?
Is it that it says something about decay ?
All this, which had inherent beauty
and contained the convictions of men,
                has survived, at least in part,
and stands to witness before the ephemeral day.

We should renew, but all the same
                    make something new.

Eat little, read much.

Take the Boulevard St. Germain —
                    and let the rest go.

The genius of France is comic : wit
                    the supreme art
of wisdom, spice of truth.

The man who had a horror of whores
                        was all right
till he discovered he was married to one.

In Paris you can eat very little on very little ;
            or you can pay a lot and get even less.
Un petit peu de tout.

In making love, beauty's of no moment,
                unless you need an aphrodisiac.
Love your wife.

Prostitutes walk on the rue des Capucines
                    ("Où sont les Capucines ?").
In Montreal some saint could hardly be missed.

To a tourist, the distinction between *jeune fille* and *fille*
                is hard to explain.
Like telling a hungry man the sex of a fish.

But sitting in a clean restaurant,
watching the postcard salesman operate below
                his miserable unsuccessful traffic,

I regret my words to the man outside of Notre Dame
                                    who offered me the nudes :
"Tu m'vends ça ici ?" His eyes chickened, and he fled.

The French love honor, and fair causes,
                and name their streets after admirable men.
Even the skulking evils honor virtue,
                and unhappiness is their tribute.
As you once said : "Who am I to 'forgive' ?"

Children, fishing chairs out of the pond,
                                    do not know evil.
"Who could have thrown them in ?"

Nudes, with their sad beautiful bodies
                — as if desire had lost its savour
or had become a snare
                        to a void life.

In the vulva, you cannot discuss philosophy.

"I can't see Henry Moore at all."
"Maybe you're looking at the holes."

Abdul had ulcers, but he laughed them off.
Said he was going on to Berlin to have them out
                then continue his voyage.
Travelling for an Indian firm ;
                lonely after his wife.

Come to India, he said, and we'll put you up —
                        nothing shall be spared.
I left a note for him with Air France.

"Ludwig, don't shout," yelled the father. "It's bad form."
                But he went on that way
and wrote Nine Symphonies.

As for prostitutes, what's wrong with them
                        if they make their living that way ?
Most women do.
            And isn't it just fine ?

As for sleeping with the first comer
                        what man deserves scorn ?
(Or is money vile ? Then don't eat ! Don't drive your car !)

If you can sleep with one, why not sleep with any ?
                        (Jesus loved us all.)
Or put it this way,
in Paris even the prostitutes are chic,
and a lot more inwardly (morally) alive
                        than most of your well-bred girls.

I suppose, that prostitutes have a bad reputation
                        gives some of the less pretty girls a chance.
Yet some people are unhappy in any job.

Of course, a handshake was once the seal of friendship ;
            it's a pity to make it an act of trade.

Take marriage ...
When the goods are of a poorer grade
                        they have to go at a cheaper price.
Buy outright, use any time, service included.

And then, you will find this problem in modern novels —
how, in the meeting of bodies,
                        we are still apart.

I would have everybody do freely what is best —
and what is best
            takes no persuasion, only a demonstration.
Even a bit of art will do.

I'm looking for the key
                        (Rodolphe, holding her hand).

Sitting in a café, reading the latest canard,

I seem to know the streets, the habits, the amours
                — even the Algerian passions.
Even *l'absurde.*

A kind of hedonism is the flower of culture.
                To do nothing
                        is the end of man.

Maybe it's better not to get that far.

Said the dentist after fixing the tooth :
                "Thirty francs. It was a very big hole."
(He was certainly looking at the hole.)
It wasn't so big before you started, I said.
                I'll pay for the piece that's left —
that's all you saved.

The more serious you are, the French say,
                the less serious you will be.
You get to the point where you laugh.

A hilarious toothache !
                C'est la vie.
La joie pure. La poésie.

At a small café by the Seine
                with an armful of new books lying before me
                                — is the world so sad
Euphrosyne, city of pleasure,
                a girl with a boy at her side ...
(You see them everywhere, "Eros and Psyche")

What would it all mean if it weren't for lovers,
                the young, with love in their eyes ?
And where would we get the language of paradise ?

A city where love is fostered and made easy
                makes all day labour light.
Even afflictions seem to wait for some delight.

"And people come to Paris for the weekend," as the English
                                                    lady said.

The Greeks could see a god and say,
                    "Why, it's only a man."
But we, who know only men, want to see God.

In the church which is already music (Notre Dame),
wrapped in many coats against the grim cold,
                    we heard the Requiem of Brahms.
The old cathedral seemed to shake
        so that we feared for the glass in the precious windows
when the music of the sopranos and the bass
            combined in solemn chorus
                        with strings, flutes, and brass.
And when the Requiem was ended,
            why did no one applaud ?
Because to praise men is foolish who have praised God.
There is something more than man, we all know it,
            that like a Requiem silences human applause.

But then we have the Eichmann trial.

Eichmann is not important
            and those who are now dead no longer suffer.

(Four thousand children shipped from Paris,
taken from their mothers, hungry, hurt, sick,
sleeping on sacks, on floors,
                    in September,
screaming, to the cold freight cars,
                across Germany, Poland,
to Auschwitz.
            They no longer shriek or suffer.)

Those millions, beaten by truncheons,
                    scarred by surgery,

who ran with bleeding feet, do not suffer.

They are dead now. They are gone.

Hitler could not take from them that final good.

They do not suffer.

It is we who must think of them still.

And Beethoven will be forgotten, and Goethe,
          and the great mind of Kant (when Germany is gone)
but men will say : *They did this.*

The living are not "responsible" !
It is not a matter of blame !
          (No man is to blame for what another did.)

But monumental good and monumental evil
          are the twin realities whereby we exist...
And great evil outdarkens all good.

We may commit that crime
which will destroy all the good deeds of mankind.
'What others did' marks the way ;
          is both an invitation and a warning.
It shatters our life — of small fears and aims !

I met a very pleasant German girl, with her parents,
          on a visit to Paris for a few days.
We talked over the table. I walked her home.
She expressed herself with difficulty in English.
Who thinks more of Auschwitz, she or I ?

Who visits the Louvre ?
          Or who owns the Parthenon frieze ?

The sea belongs to whoever sits by the shore.

Say it again. What happened
is nothing to the millions dead, who suffered ;
nor are the living to blame.
(In a hundred years, or two hundred, this will be plainly true.)
The action only exists, and is real, apart from the men
who know it, or have a part in it,
          as a measure of what we can still do.

If we end the world, in what would be the greatest crime,
it could only happen because we had already prepared for it
               with earlier committed crimes.

("This could never have happened in 5000 B.C.")

All evil begins with the first crime,
               and just as the good has grown
so the magnitude of evil grows.
The Massacre of the Innocents began with the murder of Cain.
And the palaces of art are filled with tortures and knives

as well as Saints and Madonnas with gentle eyes.

History is an explosion of the human heart.

Put it
that the power to do good is always equal
                    to the power to do evil,
and we have never stopped doing both.

France is the conscience of Europe.
One considers these things :
                    Camus,
L'Affaire this-or-that,
               or the current news.

Where the best men are political
               (not that the political are best)
and even journalists can think.
"Head leather," the French call the scalp.

Of course, Hitler thought he was doing good —
               "everything is relative".
And "who are we to judge" ?

I put it to you, gentlemen,
                    draw the conclusions !
(Can you hear Mrs. Grundy's applause ?)

But only those who break the laws make the laws.
"The moral law within us" — though we must dig for it
          through the crust of Mrs. Grundy's laws.

It's odd how we fear the unknown
                    more than anything known.
As Rilke said, ". . . it disdains to destroy us."

Several times, I said, "I have lived.
          If I die after this I am satisfied."

It is not a shadow.

The secret of translation :
                    English Spoken
                    Se Habla Español.
From gods to men.
The world, the language of God.

And a flower of the aristocracies, Beaumarchais,
with a democratic touch —

now so lovely in the buttonhole
of violent "committedness"
                    and le Néant —

his graceful prose, better than poetry,
                    if any at all exists, in our time.

Translated,
all the past is translated, carried on.

So naturally the women's cathedral,
                              Galeries Lafayette
a department store with a glorious dome
and operatic golden balconies
          leading from the perfume counters
                              to the haute couture,
Le Style Méditerranée of the moment —
                    the ultra-modern text
in a familiar language, requiring no translation.

And the artists, they say, reside in Montparnasse,
trying to escape the tourists.

They've even translated Homer into hip,
                              Mozart into bop.
You sometimes wish we could work back.

But the greatest art is only a translation
                    (an irreversible continuum).
We must go on !

Who am I, wandering about the world ?

The failed traducer —
                    vain idealizing peacock —
who crystallize all things spontaneously.

Or empty realist ...

Yet there is one who looks with warm detachment
                    out upon the world,
and would create, out of that fury and violence,
          an order and a beauty that is all his own.

The Regent diamond of France.

2

When you walk down the gallery in the Louvre
                    through the fifteenth century
you can see the struggle of Venus and the ascetic Church
fought out in the artists :
                    Saint Sebastians
with tortured, arrow-pierced bodies
                    beside the allegories of Venus,
                              and music, and lust.
The Virgin herself turned sensually beautiful
so that she can be mistaken for the goddess of Love.

Poems, paintings, sculptures
                    come from the inner self —
the history of painting is a history of religion.

The same, and always new —
                    as Delacroix's 'Chopin' resembled me !

To be interesting
            you've got to have the energy
to look and to listen.

But I am Prometheus, and I have liver trouble.

The life in the streets on a Sunday morning,
with healthy young lovers off to a spring outing,
children hopping in a row, elbows like flying buttresses,
an old man walking painfully, knowledge of death in his eyes ;
a woman, face wrinkled with misery, passing,
and more lovers, and more children . . .

Sausages at the market
            au Salaisons du Petit Trou

Liberté, Egalité, Fraternité
                    has faded from the churches . . .

Think of the early Christian frescoes
in the corner of the Roman Forum,
              their simple muddy religiosity,
against the architecture of Notre Dame.

The early Christians lived in a world of darkness
                              expecting God
as a sudden millenium.

They learned later to celebrate
                    beauty eternally present,
as in the rosaces of Notre Dame.

Motorboats on the Seine ? Piscines ?
          Fresh virgins in front of Notre Dame !
                    (take your choice)
Most of us go for the girls, but the church is something else.

In the early Christian frescoes ...
          the world and God were very far apart.

There must have been a great power
in a teaching that could destroy Praxiteles.

Two old people on the sidewalk, man and wife,
          a small waggon beside them loaded with cartons.
They were there at eleven, they are still there at five.
They have no home, just sit there all day,
                              on Sunday,
waiting for the next day's work, at Les Halles.
I've seen them eat their hard bread
                    out of gnarled hands.

And Luis told me about people dying in the streets of Shanghai
without anyone paying attention ;
beggars who open their sores with knives
so that they may beg ;

and generals who always impounded the supplies
                    sent by American relief.

The extent of suffering is limited
                    by unconsciousness, or death,
in many cases.

A kind German lady offered me the Buxtehude program
                    with a pleading hand.

The quarrels of nations
            are of a piece with the quarrels of individuals.
If any two quarreled the way that nations quarrel
            it could not be adjusted by new terms & conditions,
but only by a change of heart.

You may be right, Figueras, the people
                    in the end, may bring an end to war.
But we know what is more probable.

And you are going to S. Africa
                    with a gun at your holster
for a life of peace, and a passport.

I look at workaday Paris (les Halles)
                    tough as a cormorant
gathering in the dead flesh.
Reality, as in Rembrandt, hangs on a hook.
And we try to change it.

The universe is never finished. Evil
                    is never finished. We are working
to remove it.

Yet one finds people reading their horoscope
                    or studying a flower-pot that tells the time.

La démocratie des petits
in the parc Montholon
teaches how to share the same sandlot.

If art is not only a matter of organization,
maybe politics is.

Let's not get all mixed up : HARTOUT —
LES PÂTES FRANÇAISES À L'ITALIENNE

Like the Russians winning the world
with an American idea.

I've even heard that they have four classes on the railways !

But then, that's not American.
America is practically
a classless society. Considered "brutal imperialism".

Think of the gentle Soviet tanks in Hungary :
"the iron kindness of the Russian coast"
as Patrick once put it (straight out of Sholokhov).
They keep it a secret.

In Paris the French have a way
of putting their great monuments
at the telescope end of streets.

"Ah-h ! C'est beau l'amour quand c'est bien fait !"
yells the hawker at the market, selling garlic.
People come to him, just for that.

Yet how the labours of every day destroy us !
The drag of traffic, and the monstrous routine
in all these faces !
As if the shadows on which the great sketch was painted
took mastery over the forms
of flesh, crown, and angels !

We are fools, that say in our heart there are only shadows.

And we have made our world a realer hell
than the old priests ever believed in,

an unending night-agony of the spirit,
                    unrisen, groaning under a stone.

We see only shadows
and the shadows take the shape of forms,
a world of smoke, trailing in the wake of fire.

How do we know, in a face, or cut stone
                    that they are real ?
Why is darkness terrible ?
(Are the flowers eternal names ?)
Dirt, foetor, and discordant noise —
                    are the furnishings of hell !

But if hell is real
            is not paradise also real ?
And is there no way to find it ?

A white new moon
            floated along the light blue sky.
I opened my mouth and
saw a beautiful girl walking with a tall black boy
                    holding hands.
They went that-a-way !

(The moon, also, vanished
                    over the choppy rooftops of Paris.)

And went to hear Menuhin,
                    maybe another way
out of the Metro, into an Alhambra of sound.

But caught by a continuous thread
            making an intricate design, that covered heaven,
ended bemused, entangled, in mid-air.

And fell back into Montmartre
among the gridirons and three-cornered squares

the café bars and dim hotels
               and sad soliciting girls
(and a man throwing up his guts on the sidewalk
          after a good time).

Yet paradise is here or it is nowhere...
In streets of night and morning,
and men broken by labour,
and the mountainous loom of daylight
              filling the dark night.

Here or nowhere,
among the people empty of light.

The world's most beautiful city,
           unless as they say, Buenos Aires...

And you will see genuine writers
             interviewing movie stars :
Alberto Moravia...
and Simone de Beauvoir
      writing a book on Brigitte Bardot.

Even dead ones. Poor Gary Cooper,
he had to die and he knew it.
       (Lucky for us we don't have to die,
or we don't know it.)

There was a time in my life
       when I wanted to make a master diagram
of all that is or ever was,
all the processes, manufactures, all knowledge —
         to know them, to fill in the gaps.
But life is too short. Youth is too short.

There are perhaps some short-cuts.

Pagnol says the sandy subsoil of Paris
                                    awakens the wits.
I haven't seen the soil, there may be something to it.

(In the next decade great poets will die like flies
            it's just a matter of arithmetic.)

Consider existence as a sort of amnesia.
We don't know who, or what, we are
            but construct a new life out of our ignorance.

Mind is real — it is all we know —
                    and matter merely a conception.
What is death, but an unimportant transfer, a denudation ?
Think of yourself as an eternal existence
undergoing this fiction
                    for a purpose —
no doubt, to see what you will do with it !
If you like, a creative experiment.
There is no reality, here,
Whatever there is, we make it.

Whatever it is, since there will be others after us
                    (by some necessity),
it is important that they should not be lost ;
that we discover, add to, do whatever helps
                                    to enlighten them,

to find, in the initial darkness,
            — what, if not the final reality ?

Curious, that Communist Russia excels
in classical ballet, and new orchestral scores,
                    the old aristocratic arts,
while America shapes the young (even in Moscow, in Rome
            with jazz, and musical comedy.

There is only one Revolution, and America had it first.

Do the gods stand behind the shadow world
and say, find us, imitate us
                    recreate us without seeing us ?
No, it is we who create the gods
and tell them to perfect us,
                    to recreate us, in their image.

While behind the gods there is something further still
                    that shines, gleaming and unimaginable,
like a beautiful secret, gift-wrapped in silence.

When I was a boy, going to church,
I had a vow that doubt would never assail me.
But then a new assurance came.
The hard, tentative truths.

I do not want belief.

Doubt, in any case, is good,
                    given the desire to discover.
And I need no vow, if ever I go to church,
to hold me to what I am there for.

At school once, through a window, I saw an aeroplane
as the class was breaking, and I cried out.
The teacher stopped me, and kept me ; I can remember
walking down the corridor, later,
                    through the empty playground,
looking up at the sky. There was nothing.

I had a recovery from a great headache one evening,
                    it was in the country,
the sky a pale blue, and the air cool and fragrant.
The whole world was suddenly renewed.

Then a dog was killed on the highway
and a boy wanted to take a gun
             and go out, and commit murder.

And two farming men
             faced each other with upraised pitchforks
in a quarrel over some cows.

And there was a priest who handed out candy.

I grew up, into some kind of manhood.
Ladling out water at a bucket-brigade
                         at a great fire,
one day, seeing a church burn,
I saw how little can be saved.

And had a friend with whom I shared everything.
And a girl, aged eleven,
             with long golden hair.
On the skating rink you took her hand
and went round and round.

Some of the things we lose are better than what we find.
And we think the best must be copies of the life of a child.

But childhood itself is only a copy
             of some unimagined joy —
most of it tears, at imperfection.

There is no man but lives in the shadow
                         of an infinite good,
despite all cruelty and crime.

What implanted in us such desires ?
Was it a chance variation produced in the chromosomes
by an action of 'waves' ?

The comic *wave-theory* of matter !

Accidentally turning out
          cathedrals, cantatas, and men !
Truly, we must begin again.
Go back to school, back to your desks, gentlemen,
and try again.

If we do not have religion, we must at least have philosophy.
Or the unexamined life will become unlivable.

Le néant — est en nous.
As for the little ones, teach them how to be happy —
          it's their religion.

This morning, at breakfast, I watched my late father
          sitting across the hotel dining-room.
A perfect likeness, there was no difference.
               I smiled, he smiled back to me.
In fact, we were always a bit distant.
          Nearer, he would not have seemed so real.

Death is a comfortable easy thing,
          despite all this "rage, rage"
and affirming talk.

"La conscience, c'est notre moi.
          Elle perdue, que reste-t-il ?"
Nothing, of what we know.

In the Paris Métro I met a Canadian girl
          who owned a monkey, for a pet.
Le néant est en nous.
That's why we are like gods,
          being given chaos,
the freedom to create — all or nothing.
To invent man, in every lifetime.

A game of "find the god" —
        like pinning a tail on a donkey
(difficult, when the arse is right off the wall).

We all carry within us
        a caricature of our external selves.
It's the principle of all buffoonery.

Nous sommes déçus
par la distance où nous sommes du vrai héroïque.

A work of art in its own time
        is seen in the light, from the front,
coming toward us, with all the past behind it ;
later, it is seen far back, in shadows,
                behind all the others.

What happens when suddenly
        everything appears small ?
Every desire for glory has drained away.

How could the world become a cheap thing ?
It must be that I am tired, poor,
        and don't want to pay the price.

Like a beggar who looks at discards
        I study the cheap looks, cheap clothes
of the Sunday crowd. I am at home with rags.

No rhetoric.
The inflation of ideas has devaluated that coin.

Every effort to say O is greeted with *blague* !
Only beggars and clowns get applause.
Because no one is rich.

The exchange is blocked with bad coin. Nazis thrive.

There's a kind of emptiness in the city streets,
        as if it were for a sabbath
when there is no God.

Tout doit passer. Le petit cauchemar.

It's hard to make a good book
that a young man might enjoy over his lunch
                        sixty years later ...

Try to change the world ...
Not to change, but to break through the glut of bad change,

to "the power and the glory" that is always there.

Though walking with a girl, one arm around her neck,
with a transistor radio hung at his wrist,
                        the boy escapes it.

There are many sides to "the real thing".
        Practically, it's what you need,
it's anything you like.

Now that we no longer believe in their God
perhaps the persecution of the Jews will cease.
It takes time.

The Jews have followed Christ
                        all over the world.
Because he is really their god, not ours.

If everyone gave him up
        they would probably take him back, as their own.
As if we started worshipping Louis XIV
                — the French would never get over it.

These artificial differences !
The question is who are the real Jews.

You little christians !

One could whisper of the pure spirit
but the pure spirit is smoke.
It was to set fire to the real it came among us.

What I hold against Jesus
          is that he ascended again into heaven
and left us here to "believe".

Left Lautrec, and Daumier, among the ashes,
and Baudelaire with an evil eye —
          Prometheus on cold embers !

"I spit at the gods," he said, "because they are distant from us."

The gods are infinite desires.
When they are pitched so high
          that we can no longer attain them
they take up a separate existence ...

Leaving us, for contrast, small shivering sparrows.

So God died, of too much perfection.
We must begin again.

3

All the infinities, perfections,
          ecstasies, all magnificence —
belong to man.

He was to be perfected, praised, desired,
          loved forever and glorified !

Let us go out to look for handsome athletes,
happy lovers, poets at café tables
          (even statesmen and business managers),
wise teachers we have not seen
          who are not in the clouds ;

e.g., a brass-plate cleaner oiling his elbows
        or singing workmen on a high rigging ;
even an efficient traffic cop.

(No men in armour, no equestrian statues.)
A "business lunch" may be a beginning —
                with facts and figures
(you, Ron Everson)
The Champs Elysées for Elysian fields,
            Mount Royal a seat for kings.

Hell is a human place, but so is heaven :
the whole Comedy at our doorstep.

Look, the king of Belgium
        riding past the Grand Palais (shadows of royalty)
                with De Gaulle.
Hurrah !
Enthusiasm shakes the crowd.

The three eternities : we have within us
                a paradise of contemplation.
(Do we need proof that hell is possible ?)
We need all three.

"Qui sont les plastiqueurs ?" asks Sartre.
(Qui sont les justes ? les vrais ?)
At lunch-time you see women
        lugging a bottle of wine and a loaf of bread.
Between rich people taking their sunbaths
        and the poor eating sandwiches,
there's a purgatory in the middle.

Politically speaking, the uncommitted —
                the danger zone.
Ask for the king ! the possibilities !

Around l'Etoile is the part of Paris I dislike,
        rich slums (though there are always good people).
Let the pseudo-paradise be dissolved !

There is the heaven of Montparnasse.
And the old heaven of Notre Dame.
And a new heaven, broken, waiting to be gathered.

How common in daily use is hell !
We're not supposed to believe in the devil !
As though our hell were here, our heaven there,
                    and all between an emptiness.

Modern man believes in hell, certainly,
but not in any good, nor any possible salvation.

He takes the literal meaning : 'Dante's Inferno'.

But there is waking that is like sleep,
                    a reverie, without argument,
a pure perception.

Allness.
Amo. An open door.

Like a long thought, a sweet remembering, without words.
All-over light everywhere. A gentleness.

There is act, gift, without afterthought.
            (Do it and run, don't look back !)
A real exception.

No ugly face.
Beauty without desire. Love without action.
            A perfect reward.

I shall creep in.
I shall lie waiting.
I shall look for a chance.

There, they are waiting for us !
Who ?
            Everyone !
                    Oh, hurry !

The butterflies are dancing (lights on the Seine)
spilling a box of feathers.
Bulles Bleues.
Someone forgot his clothes !
O joy !

They are all running together.
Is it love ?
Who cares !
Yes !

Look at the lovely banner :
                                        ABANDON
(I can't read)

Abandon something.
It looks like they've abandoned it.

(Don't laugh. It can happen to you.
I hope it will.)

There isn't a soul left in the city.
They're all up there.
What a celebration !

Paradise, is it ?

We take our heaven in small doses.
It's safer that way, for all concerned.

"Berkeley in his youth described the *summum bonum*
and the reality of Heaven as physical pleasure..."

Time floats like an island
                        in the sea of being.
We must study
its birds and flowers as language
            that tells us our past and future.
For there is no other knowledge.

Think of the idiots who want a "vision",
            having the sun-blasted world before their eyes.
It has been given !

WYNNE FRANCIS
49 BALLANTYNE SOUTH
MONTREAL WEST (QUEBEC)
H4X 2B1

We have only to read the signs.
What would it be to me if I heard voices
             (I hear your voice) ;
What if I saw a spirit
             (when I see your face) ?
It is impossible not to read the signs.
The very eyesight speaks, and the ear sees,
while all the visionaries grope in the dark.

We do not see ;
as greatness does not know itself —
Rousseau and Voltaire facing each other in their tombs,
             under the Pantheon.
Voltaire who "would not go on all fours".
Rousseau, who chided wit.

An opaque mountain of books
             stands between man and man.
Yet all the senses read
             in the knobbled braile of things.

My favourite reading place in Paris
             was a small park
by Saint-Julien-le-Pauvre
with the old church at the back
             and the cathedral in front,

the traffic passing by, and children at play
             (new ones asleep in their mothers' arms),
and languid lovers on the shady seats, holding hands.

A beautiful woman on a bench
             with a line of cars behind her.
The hedge, the fence, the trees
             like a poem on a page.

But actually the trees speak an older meaning :
I look at the wandering trunks, the leaves,
             the dark serenity of silence
that no one in the city sees.

There are people who think of books only as "dirty stuff".
"The kind of thing you get in books."
And of course there's the trade in "the nude" :
NE NUS JAPONNAIS etc.
(To cure us of it, everyone should walk naked for a year.)
It's an old metaphor, the world as a used book.
Read it literally — keep God out of it —
or read between the lines.

E.g., the Sainte Chapelle,
— no need to insist on the beauty of fireworks.
You can "see" God.

No one has to affirm life,
we hold on to it desperately enough.

I suppose part of all beauty, like a clean slate
or a new canvas,
is the pleasure of knowing it can be spoiled.
The promise of untried experience.

(There is also the courtesy of the audience.
One should applaud a little
even if the work is not very good.)

As pure art, it is Psyche —
the ballerina's butterfly body.
For what is spirit
if not the potentiality of things ?

(Not the supreme good of the Soviets, the state
as the superego.
"Don't look under my skirt," the Iron Curtain,
or self-righteousness that cruelly castigates the child.)

Inono no vaovao ("What's new ?")
Raphia, Aleurite, Sisal,
Ylang-ylang, vanilla, lemon grass.

"Inevitable communism" says my friend.

A problem for psychoanalysis, all politics
is a problem for psychoanalysis.

In crisis, an incipient psychosis.

We read the wrong meaning. Mostly
                    a misuse of mind.
Piss has corroded the sidewalks of Paris.
What sort of poetry is that ?

DANS CETTE MAISON HABITA
What is it ?

      Cabaret   Music-Hall   Dancing

JOCKEY

"ON S'Y AMUSE"

A tragi-comedy, mock-romantic realism.
L'absurde.
          Or comic surrealism...
An infinite défilé of the finite.
A puzzle with private answers.
An opportunity.

In the Cimetière Montparnasse
          Sainte-Beuve
          Laurens
          АЛЕХИН
          Coppée

LA COMMEDIA È FINITA

Some of the names illegible.
Or so new, they died "en déportation"
                    in Germany, or Poland.
"Love one another."
"Les morts sont invisibles, ils ne sont pas absents."

Yet we either want to learn it from great men
or have it handed to us
          by "an ordered society".

It is really each man's business —
        with taste, toast, monkey, or mistress.
"Let's see what you can do now."

There's some bit of satisfaction
        that eternity must extract
even from every human failure.

The statistical chaos is a soup-pot of succulent cooking.

Imagine a subway-stop called
        MONTPARNASSE-BIENVENUE
And almost in every train there are lovers standing
        practically doing the works in public.
"Je n'entends pas par là ce que vous appelez en France l'amour,"
        said Arthur Miller to the interviewer
                (probably travels by taxi),
while in America "sex is the only thing real".

There is no doubt that Soviet Russia represents for the world
                                                today
        what America did in the last century
("Air from the Caucasus" in their Métro).

Here a man lies curled up on the griddle
        with a bottle beside him :
PRIMIOR Notre Vin Quotidien.

CRICKET : name for a cigarette lighter.
NECTAR : a pure-bred pony
        whose father was Rantzau and mother Frieda
        (a thing of beauty)
And we try to sew together the human body
        and whatever else it is made of,
but cannot do it.

Mem. A permanent address book for great men.
Voltaire, Marie-Arouet. Panthéon No. 1.

There's a kind of ideal beauty
        O so frail and powder-pale
The food of poets

Miss millefeuille, not a promise of experience
                              but of pure heaven
(in the shuttle, between sex and love).

For the Greeks, it wasn't man's body that was beautiful
but the god in man that was beautiful.

Most of what we see is absurd.

Now the novelty is gone. And now that the place is familia
                and real, it can tell us nothing.
Only the unfamiliar and unreal
continually become, or promise to become — real.

The fact that one is leaving
                makes it even more unreal.
Adieu, ma belle.

Happy the man who has some world he loves,
                        that he can call his own,
to which he can return.

Like the waitress in the café
                hugging her mug of café-au-lait,
to whom the streets belong, the street markets, the shops,
                                        the mer
                and life is a round of genial affairs.

Without it there is no *beau voyage,*
                        only homelessness,
a world of strangeness that is not a place.

Adieu Paris.

"Ta bouche est comme un sandwich très délicieux.

"Je cherche tes puces.
"Il n'y a rien, rien. C'est le néant.
"Il faut changer notre vie."

"Mais les Américains ont acheté le monde, hélas,
"avec le drapeau rouge à cinquante-quatre plis."

"On a trouvé hier soir
"un poète noyé dans une bouteille de Coke."

Where are the gods, in the dreaming stone
The Cnidian Aphrodite
                    of transfigured desire

The gods are not invented, they are discovered
                    and rediscovered !
(Though Christianity was once a fierce fanatical madness
          destroying gods and temples.)

See how the Egyptians made pictures speak...
a true language, saying we did this
              like this, would catch fish
          row, hunt fowl, lead cattle,
                        carry goods,
                              like this, like this !

But Egyptian gods are dead
              and Greek gods are living still.

Venus, the love that ennobles the body.
Apollo in the breathing stone.

They now exist in modern Paris,
                    city of barmen and bistros,
of bateaux mouches and métro —
                        so soon to be extinguished.
Seen for a moment, like a carnival of fireworks,
          to 'Ohs' and 'Ahs' of surprise,
                        the glittering appearances,
they vanish, leaving some paintings —
          "Paris as Seen by the Masters",
                        poems, or music,
caught in the amber of art
like dead flies, with twigs and leaves around them.

Sure it is good to be living. But we don't
         really matter that much. The permanent matters.
Something that art reveals.

There are no short-cuts to it. Time
         is the main highroad to eternity.

The tender vanishing life,
evanescent shadows playing
         over the gay straw hats, young faces —
as the French Impressionists captured life on the wing.

From the High Renaissance to the nineteenth century
painting adjusted its forms
         (beginning with myth and divinity)
until it had found the actual, real,
in the immediate moment of living.

But a moment is brief.

And no sooner had they found it
than the mystery vanished in formal vision,
         a spray of lights, or a cloud of shadows,
or just paint flashing across a screen.

Now they are far away and more remote than ever
         from the sensual present.
And they have gone to the secret processes
                           of nature,
that makes form, out of whirling chaos, and energy,
the place of the unborn, titanic powers.

What we want in art, as life, is the numinous present.
Gods, a secular Apollo.
         Aphrodite.

She says that desire can be noble.
But they have hated desire, and have destroyed beauty,
so that no one was there to tell them
                           desire can be noble.
And therefore desire became ignoble.

Now that we want to believe in desire,
     we say, "Venus is desire . . .
               Venus is the goddess of love."
But Venus is not the goddess of love.
Venus is the divinity of desire,
and nothing is more hateful to her than ignoble lust.

"Desire can be noble," she says.
And that is why it is not easy
      to honour or to worship Venus
           (no more than any other divinity),
for she would have you improve your character,
and every virtue,
so that even chastity is sometimes part of her ritual.

III

*"This earth is honey for all beings, and all beings
are honey for this earth."*

THE UPANISHADS

1

The soil of England, June flowers
                              in the bright sun,
daisies and purple vetch,
and soft sheep nibbling in the shade.

Ramshackle huts in the allotments,
                  old country homes by the road.
Even the weeds are domestic on this billowing land
        of soft contours, small valleys, brackish streams,
and lawns like one continuous golf course.

My stepmother country.

The wall of matter like a heavy stone,
a cliff of habit and accustomed repose...

Can the common day
                  shine with transcendence
so that the heavens show ? I cannot say.
But here if anywhere I would unravel the heart of the rose.

Well, one would think —
You know what you want to say, why not say it ?
Or, "You've already said it !"
But it isn't that simple, or that sublime.

I have to convince myself.
What I want to say I want to see.

The point is not to say it but to show it.

Many poems have been written
but the new poem still to be written
                  is always the first true poem
on that dark eternal shore.

Here you have "Private Gardens"... "For Subscribers Only"...
                  And "You Are Requested Not To".
Even the roses are heavy with grime.

But there is enough space in Kensington Gardens
for those who do not need to be alone to be alone.

And the roses are heavy with time.

In the evening hour,
when the cobbled lane is empty of traffic
        and the neat housewife sprays the hanging flower.
From each black enameled door, in the silent street,
the shadows steal away, on catlike feet.

This morning, at Hyde Park there was no one spouting.
And even my Angel was taking a rest
                in the humane shade,
so well had the bent spirit of love provided for the people.

But "now another look at that instant of death,"
                        said the announcer
when the Japanese Minister was assassinated.

In the movies they had it in slow motion.

Compassion, said Arthur Miller, is what men need
                but do not understand
(2000 years, yet no one understood).

Love... for the small dog, the hungry rabbit, the wild
                                        mustang..
or you cannot even love a woman.

No one understood.

They thought it was about "the battle of the sexes"
                                        (the misfits !

Is it that we are deprived, only to discover ?
Do we repeat, only to encourage — others ?
And each one begins in the darkness
                in order that he should find ?

The pewky common people,
       "Fings Ain't Wot They Used T'be",
give their character to the Dispatch
              Pictorial The People News of the World

their "Reynold's Please" and Sunday Times

The floods of popular culture
              threaten to sweep away Old England
what they have achieved over three centuries
                     in "the best corner of Europe".
While America is now a plutocracy
where affluence is possible to all,
and democracy is not a menace
                     to any tradition.

I gag at vulgarity
—an immigrant's son, who like work and wash-up,
       printing, against the dirt of creation,
poems or books —
                     or picket against "ugly buildings",
newspapers, stage shows.

Even quiet disapproval might do it.
We are all fearful
of the common law, of admiration and scorn.

Re Freund, dec., re Inheritance
re Meeks, an Infant
Marten v. Flight Refuelling Ltd., action.

Always some kind of failure, or catastrophe ;
yet there is still a great deal to build on.

As for truth, each lives his own piece of fiction,
              and sometimes they intersect.
The real is painful.

What is it — shone out of her eyes, that time ?
Something beyond truth or illusion,
                           that explains them.
As we leaned over the rail, the wind in her mouth,
what did she say ?

(Thalia)

"There it is —"
                    (looking far out to sea) .

A very common thing, an ordinary flower.
They grow by the road.

The leaves can't talk.

After several million years of silence
                    we begin to speak :
"I don't know."

Is everybody ignorant ? Who knows ?

We are here on some kind of surface
                           as if cut off from
whatever it is that made it,

that gave us passions :
                    we can choose
but we cannot choose what we choose.

Are we too free ?
          (They say we are not free)
It's only the mind that's free . . .

We could do with a little solid reassurance,
          a little definite information.

I suppose there is nothing to know
                    as we can know it.
I suppose it's better this way.
We are only trying to find out what we already know.

(A division of labour ...
          Do you want to operate your own bowels
with charts and mathematics ?

"Valve No. 3, open !")

The fact is, whatever we know and use
                    we're like to misuse.
Perhaps that's why we were left ignorant
                    of the most important things.

(They are now making infants in a laboratory.
And deadly bugs. And bombs.)

Carlyle said we are sick
            because we analyze
and now we must analyze, because we are sick.

Nature's fools.
The self-guiding toys of the laboratory.

(Is it a joke ?
          No, it is not a joke.
But don't take it too seriously.)

"I did not create the world."
You are not the god of the machine.
Don't even try to invent one.

Suppose that fighting cocks (with the razors)
                    came to their senses ?
Suppose they understood the situation ?

We are able to understand — too much !
Yet because it is only our work, it is nothing.

God keeps his business and ours separate.
Treats us like children.
          "All right, if that's the way you want it."
We tried for a little affection, a little communication,
                    but it came to nothing.

We could arrange our lives. We try to.
It is not enough.
                    And then, the razors !
Keep on living, says the germ.

Learn to look at beautiful women as we look at flowers.
We don't have to pick them. Avoid
                                private gardens.
The public walks are in full bloom.

Meet a friend, go to Shayer's
Spend whatever energies you use.

Very well, says the manikin, I can hardly refuse.

Ai, ai, we make chaos, or we make order.

An intelligent-looking gentleman sits beside me
                        reading a book.
Like he's no square.
You can tell by the cover.

DEAR MR BUTTERS
                    (written on the sidewalk)

        WE WENT TO
                JOIN THE ARMY
        AT YONDER
                    BARRACS
            A.P.
            B.A.
        M.J.
                F.G.
            A.B.
            E.B.

        HA !
        HA !

A little chaos is a friendly thing.

What is it makes for misuse ?
The very devil. A dram of ill.
Some function making a perturbation
          as great as the moon — a burning Vesuvius !
Freedom's packed with possibilities,
                              for evil, or for good.

Suppose, like Blake, we imagined "Jerusalem"
              — out of nothing !
Does it not exist ?
An idea is reality.
Not 'only in the mind' but in the mind.

Mind, the great orchestrator of meaning,
                    lord of all the things that are.
Matter could not be, without it,
disjoint points in a vacuum, else, of space and time.

Order, kosmos, the knowing process.
Without it there's only the flux.

One could become pragmatic. Honor all conceptions
              of nobility, as the Greeks did.
All the virtues, in their variety.
                    And never ask "Are they one ?"

Socrates deserved hemlock ! A Hebrew
          wanting a single good !
                    Olympian quarrels
sharpen the independent states of the soul.

But health is a virtue.

Recognize the good wherever it may be.

We didn't describe ourselves, poets rarely need to.
"Meet me at the corner of Oxford and Bond."
                    "Where shall we go ?"
"Somewhere to get away — from this."

Later, looked at sculptures in the chantry
                    at Worcester
damaged by the pickaxes of reformers ;
the broken nose of their king, on his tomb,
and the bits of skin, of a Dane, who had been flayed alive
for stealing a bell from the church.

All these, besides two chimneys
                    with a brick factory behind them —
tell us what we do, what we choose
that others will recognize
either as good, or an inexorable blaze.

Lovely houses, ugly houses,
                    riches or poverty build them,
and economics is the study of how things are done.
We have the goods, the machines, the people,
                    and will not produce abundance with beauty
until we direct the will of society toward it.

Demolish brick slums, sweep away the shops, the shambles,
                    to build the new city where the other was.

Reality is mostly what you like. Each man clings to his own
like a gimlet-eyed poet, seeing his private truth.

But there is also the open garden of God
                    (a very great man)
in which all things grow.

Throw it all away, he says,
                    throw it away and start again.
Your words are still only the type-casts of things.
                    Hardly real.

Today I met a man who made a kite like a huge bird
        and flew it to excite his friends ;
but it was only a grim bird of paper,
                not a real owl, or eagle, or swan.
I left him with his obsession
        and watched the green-throated ducks
in the Round Pond, swimming without a thought in the world.

We've got to look toward the tops of great trees,
the dark branches among the green, for the patterns we need.

Abba, with a child to be born,
the poet whose thoughts glisten in the dew.

Opulence, in Palace Green, once gathered meaning.
Roman proconsuls ruled half the world,
their mansions now are only shells of power,
                a consulate or abandoned ruin,
with all the glass broken, the green wild and overgrown,
                black, peeling walls.

Is power gone back to the soil ?
The Dutch build dykes against the sea,
the English have built them against the working classes.

It's difficult to love. Maybe impossible.
How can we 'love one another' ?
At best we can only pretend.
How to be able to love — anything, anyone !
                —It's the main object of life, of art.

The Oxford boy
with white collar, striped shirt, polka dot tie and dark suit
                lording it in the train
with his copy of The Times.

College boys flaunt the sham aims of their dads ;
a dungaree freedom, in America —
                girls, liquor, and cars.

Like great men, the upper classes
                suck on the myth of a 'superior being'.
Virtue costs money.

Love of aristocracy, on toilet tissue,
                Silver Silk, a coronet on every piece.

We became individuals
                to enjoy a little corner of comfort.
But the common lot is a waggon of pain.

That's why morality is an ought,
something you do for others, or for the general good.

There's a very strong religion blowing from the east.
It will blow all over the world.

Names mean nothing, capitalism can call itself communism
                Or vice versa. It already does.
The centralized life, the religion of the hive,
for a time, will replace any private good.

It's very difficult for America
                to make a gospel
out of their immoral creed.

The Marxists are now the moralists.
                We are against the common good.

But freedom will return. Men will always return
                to the sweet vortex of the "I".

Actually, communism is simply machinery
                and 'organization from above'.
It's something they've got to try.

The main thing is to save a little freedom,
to plead for "loose joints".

Dammit, friendship is only possible
                    where one submits to another
and listens to his oracle (we can take turns).
Otherwise each is his own.

We certainly don't want a common belief.

You play your guitar, I'll string my thoughts.
If we pause we'll listen to the birds.

I'm outside all dogmas. I want to observe and think.
In most things, adapt.
Though in England, you only feel at home
                    if you're well-dressed & well-heeled.

Actually, I like "anything goes" —
after a while we can pick up the good bits.

The "great good man"
                    is a scoundrel, a sham —
Romains and Eliot have him.

Does no one deserve praise?
We've got to stand naked before the world...
Ah, Rousseau!

"The Roots of Honour"!

Perhaps the reason why we contradict ourselves
                    is that we want to be open to every truth.
"Have it your own way."

I will walk under the white clouds and gigantic trees
                    until the discords fade,
until my thoughts run smooth.

The real world, one world, of birth and death.

Everything good.

2

Have you seen the weeping beech
              hanging like a green pavilion ?
Or the tulip tree
        reaching up to heaven ?

Have you seen the cedar ?
The kakee tree, the gingko, the lobed sassafras
         —have you inhaled their fragrance ?

The glistening leaf of the strong oak, suber,
        the slender white birch,
                the dappled maple,
the tough sticky pine, swelling with rosin ?
Have you sat on the moss among the brown cones ?
Have you seen the contours of the leaves ?
Or listened to the silence in their shadows,
           or the rush in high winds ?

I have gone to the green pavilion of morning
        and watched the dahlia open her eye.
I have seen the violets breathe in the blue light
          under pendent leaves.

There's a delicate beauty of India, in a ballroom dress,
and a handsome negro, to whom all about are loving and
                                friendly

There are the lovers, it is night.
By the stairs he is kissing her mouth, and she clings.

A girl practicing the violin at her window
        gives me the glad eye and a groaning note.

The paradox is that pride, which is self-seeking,
results in the most impersonal and enduring monuments,
        the great houses, and arts.

Poets like rooks follow the plow.

Mostly, people are obliged to be human
      by a certain amount of insecurity and fear.
To be just to the weak is the great test,
         like doing good without a reward.

As for Auschwitz and the other horrors
      it's not so much that the victims were Jews
but that they were human.

It has concerned the Jews too much
        and the Christians too little.

"Look after things . . .
      and turn that slave girl into cash."
(Rufus to Epillicus, 100 A.D. in Britain.)

Surrounded by sword hilts and helmets.

Utillam puellam ad nummum redigas / and the diary of
                       Ann Frank.
"Make sure that the warheads are ready—"
        top secret (2000 years later).

Even in the highest cultures, mystic India,
      there was wanton cruelty.

Though Assyrian and Egyptian gods
             reek of power,
Greek gods were delicate, vulnerable —
      their gentleness and gracefulness
        a harmonious union of the elements.

"Begin by loving earthly things," says Plato,
      "for the sake of the absolute loveliness..."

Despite all the blood of the innocent
the leaves glistened
as the still-trembling bodies fell into the earth.

About your murders nature doesn't care
      because death is not such a bad thing to her —

just a more rapid turnover.

God is a great gambler, always counting the winnings.

He never counts the chips that are gone
                    only the ones he's raking in,
millions that weren't there in the beginning.

All right, all right, everything perishes.
But what a pity to fold up the particulars
                    and yield to others !
Over and over ! The same over and over !
The particulars must go, and we are particulars ;
and will never again be, no, never again be.

Does today regret yesterday ?
Now we are today, yesterday, and tomorrow.
But who is there who is all yesterdays and all tomorrows ?

For whom all days and every day, forever, is today.

How could there not be ?
          If there would not be, nothing would be.
Is there a line without a surface ?

If all are moving, is not something still ?

They say that nothing is still.
And they say there is no surface.
Then nothing is real. It is all fiction.

But even a fiction's for someone to imagine.
We imagine a small part of it, for a small time.
Who is there who imagines all of it, for all time ?

Genocide is not a new thing,
          we exterminated the North American Indian.
The English killed off the Britons ...

There are no Neanderthal men !

Think of the more general condition of nature,
              it will save you from hysteria
and prepare you for the textbook facts.

Man is a new thing. Indifferent slaughter
                    was there from the beginning.
We have only begun to care.

A short History of Massacres could be prepared
in a week or two of research :
        China, Assyria, Egypt, Greece and Rome,

the "Story" of Carthage, of Thebes,
                    of Peru, Mexico,
Japan.

Perhaps we have now begun to care.

The Chinese are preparing to exterminate us.
                              No wonder.
Or maybe the Negroes will finish off the whites. Surprised ?
It isn't pretty but it's natural.
We're only slowly learning to care.

In fact, pity seems to be a recent idea of God's.
              Who knows ?
Maybe it's the new order he's trying to bring in.
              (He sent "His Son".)
Don't despair. The real wonder is that any pity is there !
How simple things would be if there never were.

Two thousand years ?
You can't think of history in terms of weeks.

Monkeys will watch a rhinoceros die
                    without batting an eye.
How childlike the animals are !
              The pet monkey, the dog.
As though evolution itself were a growing up.

Can we imagine the adulthood of us all ?

The gods within us, aching to be real.

Maybe they have their world
        but they want us to equal them in this one.
We must help. Act as envoys.
We have their seal and authority.

That's the wise thrush
hopping about on the newly watered ground.
Ti-ti-ti-ti-ti-ti ! (six steps and a pause)
                        Listen.
Peck ! Ti-ti-ti-ti-ti-ti ! Nothing.
Then nip ! a worm !
The wriggling thing fell out on a leaf.
                        The bird turned away.
Leave it ? No chance. Back to the worm
        —doomed thing ! He gave it a good shake.
Threw it. Picked it up. Mangled it. Jabbed.
Then flew away with the bit in his beak.

From the point of view of the worm
                it was all unforeseen.
Exit into a new world, of light, of air.
                        The end !

How could anybody grieve ? There will be other worms.
        "Feed my birds."

From the point of view of the bird
                something that happens every day :
"One of my favorite worms."
                Very good.

It was all well arranged. Till we began to mourn.
Memory. And love. And a wish to save,
                        snared us.
So that we wanted it all as permanent
        as remembered things.

Memory, our first replica of the unchanging,
                an imperfect piece of eternity.
It is a co-existence. Refusal to forget.

A first realization of death
                    (for death is only change).
Now that we have memory, now that we mourn,
               how can we accept death ?
Yet how can we be so foolish as to avoid change ?

We live divided. Sometimes not very happy.
Those who remember more
                    think most of other worlds.
Those who love, mourn.

Let us take what we have and not desire more.

The short eternity of art, of love.
                    We are not gods,
nor lucky beasts.

Someday, in the great future, perhaps
                    there will be men
no longer torn,
for whom time is one eternal now
          and change an ever-unchanging change,
who see the permanent in the impermanent
               and the same rose in every dying rose.

We have memory to will the future,
love to enjoy,
visions of perfection that we might improve.

Like a lens our thoughts focus the light
                    too near... too far
or midway between the distant and the actual
where, on the rock, the minerals gleam.

Look : "Still Life With Chip Frier"
          (every mixed-up goddam thing in the kitchen).
How about cutting a couple of holes
          in a couple of poles —
                    "The Hollow Women"?

Everything that passes is semblance for a day —
        the dirty Thames (dirtiest of rivers)
                        with all that it bears —
and the few of us look back through time
        seeing the Titians, churches, the Roman shields
and catch for a moment a glimpse of pattern
        — O not the real, not substance
                but a hint of sequence —
that others, caught in time,
        pitched from moment to moment, falling,
may find an instruction, a hope,
                a breath of encouragement . . .
But how could they cease
their watery progress to listen, to think of the emptiness
that still surrounds us, the shreds of our meaning,
        in the precipitate rush of existence ?

. . . A time for the artist to relax,
                        a time for simple truth.
To come back to the simple fact,
                to humanize his art.

Ah, Wyndham !
Cophetua may still rhapsodize
                        but at the Tate
I did not find Ezra, where he used to hang
                almost life-size.

The beard replaces the necktie,
        the pub gives way to the espresso bar.

And poetry is the fruit of experience !
The present is always present !
                        Ha ! Ha !
All you've got to do is be there to enjoy it.

The dead don't care — they're neither here nor there.
Something keeps the world always full,
                like a daily newspaper.
An atomic ticker-tape ?
                Ghost writers ?

In a corner of a London museum
I saw the ballet shoes and feather-white dress of Pavlova
in which she danced The Swan,

with old clothes, torn gloves, and bits of broken glass
from those times.

And Adelina Patti's tiara —
a triumph in La Sonnambula —
buried in a downstairs room.

Eliot's Waste Land, which we thought "the age",
is not England,
not even London,
but his own Lower Thames, down from the Bank,
that he knew so well.

If Eliot had been the young man carbuncular...

I said, there should be an increase in beauty
since there are more women than men
(only the beautiful will propagate their kind)
But then, what about ugly men ?
Maybe we could take turns...
Anyhow, hyacinth girls are somewhat rare.

Even a common beauty, on Trafalgar Square,
might please a tourist
with camera notebook in mid-air.

Thalia, ripeness is all...

I passed the house in Ebury street
where Mozart wrote his First Symphony.
People who have lived in these streets,
in this world...
And went to visit John Stuart Mill, Carlyle.

The perfect life is possible :
ducks in St. James' Pond
have it as good as could be, the state of nature
under the protection of man.

We cannot provide this for ourselves ?

Man seems to be against nature from the beginning —
                naked, he cannot live
without taking some animal's hide or building a sloppy den.
Must make it "artifical" before he can survive ...

And then there is so much choice,
              between a cave and a castle wall !

His job's to create a new nature that will imitate nature.

Society is a work of art — as haphazard,
             you might say, as this one.
It is an order, of a new kind.

And speaking of art, what could be more beautiful
         than a couple in their sixties,
             pudgy, wrinkled, with hands like brown claws,
walking down the path together, arm around shoulder,
          talking of intimate things ?

Or is it nature ? They say that marriage
             is against nature.
Wanton promiscuity ... men getting their teeth smashed,
         killed over a woman ...
Someone invented marriage.
It's certainly a work of art —
         that "imitates nature" !

There are pools of reality — the galaxies, the seas,
         the domesticities.
Snow's world and Farrell's. Or this today,
          and Elizabethan London.

While Russell talks about "dry rain".

I once wrote to Ezra, "If they explain your poem
        they'll kill it."
He answered, "Don't worry. They won't."

Ilex Aquifolium, the pale-fringed holly.
The Strelitzia like a tropical bird,
        the hanging lamp of the purple fuchsia.
The rose Spiraea and the royal lily.
(And birds come to eat from your hand —
                would you want to harm them ?)

Gleditschia   Dietes   Regal Lily

Not that the poem doesn't have a meaning.
            It's what holds the thing together,
an invisible ghost.

I have seen the parts of a flower
            floating, detached from the stem,
yet knowing somehow what to do.
Growing, drinking in rain.

Callamandra   Zantedeschia   Gloriosa

And an orange tree, with dozens of fruits

You would know from their love of flowers and birds
            the English are a gentle people.
The lady told me she turned her garden into a sanctuary
            and couldn't paint the eaves,
there were so many nests.

(Though last night I saw a man in a state of passion
            that was like a fury from another world.)

There are plants that choke their kind.
        Lilium Burbankii, tiger lily . . .

(This business of Hitlerism was like that,
            a trans-human fury,
like the heat of galaxies, incomprehensible to us.)

Even around a coffee table
            someone will break out in tears.
'To agathon, the good' is a flower of the temperate zones.

The fruit of the Magnolia of Yunnan
                    opening their great pods
and the Cashmere Cyprus of Tibet
                    that hangs like drapery, green and brown.

Nymphaea and tropical fish

But the rhododendrons were not in flower.
"The rhododendrons were not in flower!"
                    "Ah, you must come back another time."

To see the famous roses,
                    Mme. Butterfly, Sutter's Gold, Masquerade,
                    Christopher Stone, Misty Morn.

(Was it Mandeville wrote —
                    "How Roses First Came Into the World"?

Primula Japonica...

Ah, Waste Land!

3

"What's the answer?" students often ask.
From happy childhood to miserable old age —
                    what's   the   answer?

A kind of exploration.

Though young crocodiles feed on insects, older ones eat men.
When man arrives the wild animals are always threatened
                    with extinction.

The new god
                    DEOXYRIBONUCLEIC ACID
                                        (Deus, ecce deus)
When you consider the complexity of organisms
all our worries are nothing but a little surface trouble.

The rhino horn is made of compressed hairs.

Each particular life — the whole universe.
I heard a naturalist say : "Men and animals
                              cannot live side by side."
Where man is, nature is soon likely to become barren.

The point was made that man has survived
                    because the big cats don't like his meat.

We are separate universes,
                    cut off from the others.
"I love you because of your absence."

The porcelain beauty of English women
                    has been the ruin of English art.
Or maybe art shapes the women.
(To love one would be 'a storm in a teacup'.)

Beauty by artistic selection.
To love her is a liberal education ..." wrote Defoe
          of a certain Mrs. Hastings.

The next stage in evolution ?
                    Nature is working on it.
A stomach that will digest Fish & Chips.

Cf. Harmsworth —
"The public press is the concentration of all that
                    is best in thought..."

And Charles Lamb : "I love the very smoke of London...
The man must have a rare recipe for melancholy
          who can be dull in Fleet-street."

But the smoke has thickened
                    (mixed with car gas)
and Fleet Street, today, would make him melancholy
          without a recipe.

We need a smoke-proof lung possibly ?
("I made it out of a mouthful of car-exhaust.")
Perhaps the oil reserves will not last.
Only the women remain beautiful.

It's something you contain, or something that contains you.

But there are no consolations in Sigmund Freud.

Henry Moore's people, out of Dali,
and the desert ossifications of the Surrealists
                    may be prophetic.
Against which you have the complacency of the pipe-smoke
            and the man with the Reader's Digest.

The average income in Britain is $1000 a year,
                but in Burma it's about 40 (forty dollars).
World population 3 billion,
annual increase 50 million (roughly the population of Britain)

Conventional dullness, RSBA.
Yet maybe the architects are the only modern artists,
making their structures of light and efficiency —
            for the clean new life, of activity,
                    honesty, openness to fact ;
but we'd have to bring the whole world into it.

Yaws must be eliminated. Fewer people but happier.

There is so much incredible suffering
                that crucified Jesus makes one laugh
at his comfortable nails.

Pity is just a beginning.

We've bitten it off, we've got to chew.
Take biology : "The Biological Basis of Human Freedom."
                                Or look at the birds.
They're very small characters that say everything
                            (God's little aviators).
And all the man-fearing animals.

As Canaletto painted an eternal daylight
　　　　over his Regatta on the Grand Canal ;
or that foreverness in the eyes
　　　　of "A Family Group" by Lotto.

Eternal chicken, eternal bread and fruit...

The great place of art
　　　　is halfway between this world and some other :
Hals to Hogarth, Giotto to Botticelli —
　　　　including the English pantheon, Aristocracy.
But the unknown will remain unknown.

This is our gift, to extricate joy
　　　　from earthly things,
what is distilled of transcendence
　　　　out of the visible.

With Riemann, & Einstein,
with Hoogstraaten's peep-show,
and Vermeer, the fascination of symbolism.

A heap of straw, in which a needle of truth lies hidden,
　　　　Turner's "Evening Star"
　　　　　　over the sea...

The greenery of many mounting trees,
with nary a cloud, a spot of light
　　　　held in the memory.

Against pessimism
　　　la vie a connu le froid et la mort
　　　dès le commencement.

Success counts. What else matters ?
The courage of the creation against the cold.

When that is over, quiet submission, and sleep.
If we retain our identity in the afterlife,
　　　　who among us will remember that he was Caesar ?
If we remember this in another
　　　　how could we not be unhappy ?
I only love what I know.

Even what I know vanishes. How could it be otherwise ?

Do you want to abstract the birds from the trees ?
      Or will you preserve all the leaves ?

A few great men in the museums,
      like the keystones of London Bridge
or the ruins of Coventry.

Yet all that ever was is, there is only one present.
And time is the breathing spirit, the movement
      by which it speaks.

The deer walks on tip-toe.
      The seal was once a cat.

What is the zygomatic arch ?
What is the condyloid process ?

Consider the dugong and the manatee
      that feed on aquatic plants.
Or the giraffe, eating the tops of acacia trees.

There are animals you wouldn't want to meet, still in Europe
      the wildcat of Scotland,
the wild boar, the wolf in Portugal, the lynx in Sweden.

How much of it all do you want ?
      How much can you take ?

Will man be the gardener of the world
      and bring order to Eden ?

Perhaps the price is too great —
      and there is 'the will to suffer'.

Perhaps the price is always to suffer !

Perhaps it is not possible... perhaps love is not possible...

But I am satisfied. Rest awhile
      on the cushion of time, here and now,
and prepare, for whatever it is it gives.

I said to my friend, "Don't read this,
                              it'll make you dizzy."
But she read on, said she couldn't stop.
        "What is it ?"
I said : "The vertigo of freedom."

A living thing asks itself
        what milliards of years no plant, bird, or animal . . .
It was never part of their business.

Why stop at all, she said, why not go on ?

In nature, beauty is a case of and/or.
There are still the atoms, and the stars
        (and all the crude machines made by man).

"Of course I can't stop," I said.

Nature is interested in beauty, look
                        at the excess of the peacock.
It likes to try the extremes, of smallness, of size —
                        all possibilities.

Nature is a lot like man, it goes to excess.

The little children in purple jackets
        with tiny raincoats over their arms
march in the sunlight to the park.

On the grass they divest, and dance in their tunics
                Ring-a-Rosie, and Go-in-&-out-the-window
while the teacher sits close by.

So they get an education
in the ways of nature, and are nature.

Nothing is ever finished.
Hokusai, Hiroshige, Kuniyoshi
                (lightning like Japanese script)
and the Wm. Morris Co.

Modern artifacts, our Danish knives,
        lace, Wedgwood, china —
even a poet or two on the boards.
                        Jazz.

"Electronic music should go with poems."
"I'd like to try a harp and a drum."
                "An outdoor auditorium
with music tunneled underground."

"How about syphoning sea-water onto the moon ?"

Somewhere in there I see a gleam
                like the sun in the leaves,
a great, bright, fearful, beautiful bird.

Where will you find it ?
Like God, the sun does not intend to be seen.

Imagine all things at last explained !
                        Finished.
Packed in the brain . . .

What do you think we're up to ?
What do you think this is ?

Crumbs to feed the birds. A little curiosity
helpful for finding a roost.

Some of the element in which we live,
        like islands in a sea of possibility.
A burning glass that warms us
                and sharpens the distant sun.

I look at these people.
Never again to see them.

The young, and the old with their small last pleasures,
sitting in restaurants or working in shops —
                        they will be gone.

This voyage is almost over. I think
      how everything will go on here
as before. As it must. And yet I know
      that somehow I am a part of it, in it
for good — or I do not live at all.

Not an individuality but an identity,
      is what we really are.
That continues, as it lives in the body,
    in fraternity with things and men.

It is the whole reality that is always there ;
something that we are, that we become,
     that now we cannot know or share.

This is all new to me.

The half of a moon.
The sound of feet.

Should I ask that tree ?
    Listen with my ear to the ground ?
Study a flower for a sign ?

I will take it all in and wait
     until like a Univac
I suddenly throw up the sum.

This will be always true, as it is now (as all we do),
and each living thing an enameled bird
      of paradise.

There were sixty people at the High Mass in Southwark
     lost in the great vault,
their prayers drowned by the Underground.

I looked for the past in the present
    (in the Borough streets placards were out
      for "Othello" and "The Merchant"
    right by the precincts of The Globe)

139

and found it residual
like thoughts in the mind of God.

There is so little of England, half of London
        seems to be filled with Indians, Poles, Africans, Jews –
students, exiles, refugees in crowded rooms.

The proportion's increasing
so that even the present is not what you expected
           — it is partly the future.

A Persian said to me, "We're taking the place over."
And on the walls : "Keep England white."
(All right, if the whites had kept out of India, Africa
        — but for that it's too late.)

Brown is a beautiful colour.
        I'm looking forward to brown.

So many lovers on the grass, in Regent's Park,
        it's no wonder the world is packed.
Now that wars are finished, what are the people to do ?

We don't even believe in sin.

Freud came too soon.
        A little more and he would have seen
the need is not for more sex but less.

Let's at least forestall the outcome :
        if we can't bring the Oedipus into play
we must hustle on to wisdom through excess.

Very few come to Europe to find
        what I've come for, perhaps none.

Was it a mirage ? the lost continent ?
        (At least not another 'Europe' !)
I'm an optimist — though things can get pretty bad,
        as the dinosaurs used to say.
Let's make good with the good.

Old sloppy Southampton, I see,
        has recovered from its wounds.
Ruins, in fact, don't last.

England ... with the old order changing,
                              sadly reconciled
to "new apartment flats" replacing "gentlemen's quarters";
ruined aristocracy, rented estates,
and the Free Market
              drawing the proud Empire
down to the common lot.

Turning home, now that the voyage is almost over,
I know that all experience is only a progress
                    to some further goal
never fixed, never final, never to be enjoyed,
moving always toward what we rarely dreamed, and never
                                        understood.

Time is not fixed, because it is imperfect ;
            and it is perfection that all change pursues.

I remember a young chimpanzee hugging its keeper
                while he stroked it indulgently on the back.
Love leads us on. And beauty.
Toward a truth that might comfort a moaning chimpanzee.

All is vanity, yet we know what to choose from vanity
that's a piece of something perhaps less vain.

Topaz, like a tear in sunlight,
                to hang on my true-love's neck ...
It will last longer than her beauty, and with her beauty
will dangle for a little, like a star that never fades.

But those we leave behind remain in their prison
                of common daily things,
and we who leave it know
                how sad it is, and foolish,
how everything men hold to is what the voyager leaves behind.

Chelsea, and Cheyne Walk,
            where Rossetti, and Swinburne, and George Eliot lived
                    (also T.S.),
and near-by Carlyle ...

And the bank by the Thames where we walked
                    (in the 'dry rain')

I saw a graveyard where the stones had been ranged
                    along the side as a low wall,
while the space itself was turned into a children's playground
We are always trampling on the bones of the dead.

It all comes down to this life of ours
of which you have the pieces
                    right in your hands.

EPILOGUE

In the daylight of departure from the shores of light,

the sea was a white burning cloud all afternoon.

Locks hanging over the counterpane
                                    or grapes spilling
out of the bright horn.

"Light."

Only in the reflection of portholes
                                    gulls
flash across mirror, a dumb sequence.

        The sea as an escritoire.

                        That pale blue

                and violet

                        heaven.

Like dreams before they begin, a tunnel
                at the end of which a blue grotto,
silently set with shrubs, shines.

Silence, in the glass light of so much meaning
it looks like indifference, and purpose so large
                the details are left to chance.

What I think when I am alone

of the sea, the road of adventure
        — what the soul sees between two lives. Hearing
                                                    only
the plaintive seagull's infant cry.

All the animals are eccentric,
        therefore we are affectionate to them
and amused.

Too much of one thing, human.

To die, to drown, to be free
             of everything human.
A clean new beginning, a ghostly embryo.

Whispers, on the burning crystal — of things to come.

In this world, everything is immortal,
                        it merely changes.
A new form, of the same old thing !

That manifests itself in change, even in incompleteness.

Naked bodies lie on the deck, new girls,
              perfect limbs,
                        shoulders,
                                  crotch.
Clean to love.

(Sir Kenneth says a small body
             is easiest to love ...)

Also, tall rhythmic bodies
             that look sensitive to touch.
There is the soft, sweet female, of any shape,
                        and the secret inward parts
of their genesis ...

The body, embryo of love. A bare beginning.

New bodies. Cherubs.
             The promise of shapes to come.
Embryos of men.

No land. It is all a wild turbulence
                        of possibilities.
A spiral nebula. A sea of milk.

We go into darkness, into deeper darkness,
             where all embryos are shattered.

An emptiness, void of meaning,
                        a signless nil
cancelling out all mathematics.

The great zero of nature, in which the little numbers flicker
            like a halftone of nazi crosses
without significance.

Concentration camp of souls.

With gas chambers and crematoria :
            "genocide" of all mankind and all animal species.

"All these must die" — by order
            of the Supreme Authority.

A scientific experiment.

Yet "eternal not-being and eternal being are the same" —
though the ship's report says "a confused swell".

Under the sea, as over the sea,
            the weather is almost permanent.
We have escaped from land-made weather.

We have escaped from great old buildings,
            from new cities, from car exhaust,
from English gardens, Rue de l'Opéra and Via Veneto —

into the grey indifference where nothing stands,
            where only the sea moves,
that is itself nothing, and everything.

Hush. It beckons. A secret void.

And the wild pulsations ... listen ...
(I do not want the blackness of the sea
      only such knowledge as this foam, the mind, creates)
Speak to me ...

Nothing, heavy as lead.
I saw the night like a dark fury spreading its wings
            to hide the day,
under feathers of cloud black as mourning.

The dark rushing horizon seemed to flee
            to the north and south from the sunset
where the light turned, twisting, broken and grey —
            white foam, frozen feathers.

You whispered to me and leaned in the darkness
                    to hide from the evil,
saying, "Take me away, save me..."
and touched my knees, while the black water
                    swirled around us.

We must go.

Where the bios shapes the body, as we shape our dreams
                    out of memory,
into the image we need.

Look at the lineaments,
what are the parts of any woman that please ?

Someone you love, or have loved, or will love.

A mixture, that makes things new
                    out of dissimilars, making a third.

Limbo. Amorphous cloud. Alembic of nature.

(Why work in mines, said the miner, in London,
                    when I can stay in the open air ?)

There, somewhere, at the horizon
                    you cannot tell the sea from the sky,
where the white cloud glimmers,

the only reality, in a sea of unreality,

out of that cloud come palaces, and domes,
                    and marble capitals,
and carvings of ivory and gold —
                    Atlantis
shines invisible, in that eternal cloud.

An architecture of contradictions and inexorable chances
                    reconciled at last,
in a single body.

The iceberg came toward us,
              like a piece of eternity,
like a carved silent coffin, out of the night,
and stood in the shattering sea,
                    serenely still,
and disdainful, while we looked with awe
                  at its still beauty assaulted
that knew neither time nor change.

In darkness. Infinite night.

Fierce, all-devouring night,
              featureless, fearful night.
Sweet, all-dissolving night.

O love. O new bright love.

There is a drop of snow on death's car.
                    A cloud against the dark mountain.
The white of the moon.

There — is reality. A white flame.

I see my angel, flying over the water,
to the blue that's like a thin gas flame around the world.

Leave me, I said,
          spirit that rise above today and tomorrow.

Already I hear
          the creatures are laughing at my words.
No one understands. It does not interest them.

Even my anecdotes must fail.

Fragments of poetry that float on the water
              as common seaweed.
A bottle. A board.

How will I separate them
                  from the drift of snow ?
Or amanita, from the edible food ?

"Poetry is meditation."

("For the masked ball," said the professor,
　　　　　　"you should get dressed up as Buddha.")

But no one meditates.

An unfair advantage.
　　　　　The brain has an unfair advantage
over the creatures.

We have more than we can use.

One of nature's excesses.

So that these exercises exhaust the average mind.

Learn to be more practical, simple and kind.

Nothing — is always true.
In any crisis, it's the best thing to do.
Nothing — is what it comes to.
It's where we begin.
Nothing — is what we like to do.

Everything comes of nothing.
It "never faileth",
it is as good as charity — those who have nothing
　　　　　also have faith and hope.

Nothing is silent. Nothing is simple.
Nothing is left to chance !
Nothing is at the heart of mathematics,
　　　　　and number the nothing in all that is.

We come to land by a pleasant shore :
to roads, houses, people
　　　　　we have not seen a long time,
so that our dreams must be corrected by the familiar still.

Talking, gladly, of the long journey ahead.
　　　　　And all the future.

It's always a new beginning.
The real, or the unreal —
                    beginning where you are.

We meet many travellers
                    who report on the way
of hidden beauty, joy, or honour
                    in the four corners
of the lost continent.

There is the sea. It is real.

.